THE NEW AMERICAN **town house**

RIZZOLI
NEW YORK

First published in the United States of America in 1999 by

Rizzoli International Publications, Inc.

300 Park Avenue South, New York NY 10010

Copyright © 1999 by Rizzoli International Publications, Inc.

Introduction © Alexander Gorlin

Foreword © Paul Goldberger

Library of Congress Cataloging-in-Publication Data

Gorlin, Alexander

      The new American Town House / Alexander Gorlin.

         p. cm.

      Includes bibliographical references.

      ISBN 0-8478-2141-2 (hc)

        1. Row houses—United States.   2. Architecture,

Modern—20th century—United States.   I. Title

NA7208.G67   1999

728'.312'0973—dc21   99-23334

                                    CIP

Book & Cover Design by Brendan Cotter

Velocity Design (NYC)

Cover image: Ogawa/Depardon Architects,

Hilpert Residence; photograph, © Paul Warchol

Printed and bound in England

THE NEW AMERICAN town house

ALEXANDER GORLIN

foreword by **PAUL GOLDBERGER**

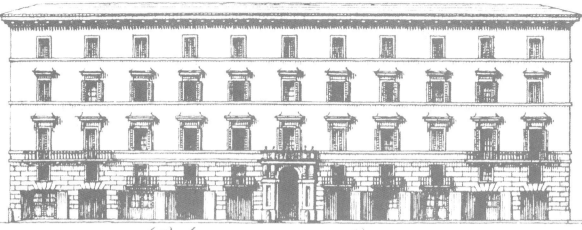

Palazzo Lozzana
sarti arch. 1834

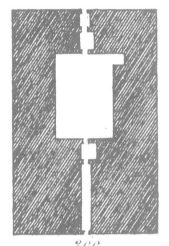

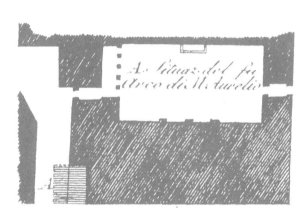

A. Situaz: del fu
Arco di M. Aurelio

200

315

Palazzo Fiano

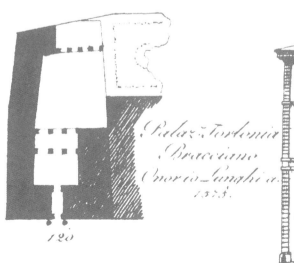

120

Palaz: Tordonia
Bracciano
Onorio Lunghi a.
1575.

Contents

PAUL GOLDBERGER

foreword

If, as Charles Eames once said, design is largely a matter of constraints, few building types come with more constraints than town houses. Alexander Gorlin describes the town house as an instance of "animated architecture within a very confined space," which concisely sums up the difficult nature of this type of building. Town houses are tightly enclosed, inevitably on sites that are barely adequate for their programs. Adjoining buildings crowd out light as well as space. The small footprint usually dictates somewhat awkward interior arrangements, with rooms often piled up vertically. There is almost never more than one facade to design, and even that, given the restrictions that apply in many urban areas, cannot be designed with total freedom.

Yet somehow, despite the relentlessness of these constraints—or because of them—the town house form has yielded a remarkable amount of worthwhile, and sometimes even important, architecture. Alexander Gorlin proceeds from the belief that the town house, for all that it flourished in Georgian London and nineteenth-century New York, is also very much a building form of the twentieth century, and indeed, that it has undergone a significant revival in the last generation, as the century draws to a close. Architectural historians have tended to overlook town houses in recent years—town houses do not, after all, create the fabrics of large cities any longer, as brownstones did for an older New York. Most of the town house designs worthy of architectural note today are either single-family, custom-designed projects or small groupings of infill projects. In an age that has come to value architectural expression highly, it

isn't surprising that the freestanding house in the country or the suburbs gets more attention than the town house tightly confined by an urban street.

And yet, paradoxically, ours is also a time that has come to value urbanism, if only in reaction to the International Style's anti-urban attitudes, and it is through the town house that the ethos of urbanism demonstrates its strength and its potential. Some of the most promising material in this book are those groupings of houses, like those by Jonathan Segal in San Diego, Mark Mack in Venice and Daniel Solomon in Los Angeles that attempt to employ the town house as a way of establishing a sense of urbanism where little or none of it had previously existed, thoughtfully and earnestly using the town house to reassert the importance of the street, and to stake a claim for the idea that in a city, the whole is worth more than the sum of the individual building parts.

All town houses are either parts of groups or individual works, either buildings that were designed as elements in a larger, multi-building composition or buildings that were designed to stand alone. Historically, American town houses that contained any significant degree of serious architectural intention have more often been of the second type—American individualism in the nineteenth century, for example, never took to the notion of the town house grouping, and instead looked kindly on the extravagant houses of New York in the gilded age, on the premise that Richard Morris Hunt's grandiosity, even though it yielded buildings that often looked more like villas dropped on urban street corners than true town houses, felt right for New York's unbridled ambitions. While there were certainly some distinguished architectural groupings, such as Alexander Jackson Davis's Colonnade Row on Lafayette Street of 1833, or the eighteen houses of limestone and red brick on West 74th Street of 1904 by Percy Griffith, or Rafael Gustavino's six houses of bright red brick and white stone trim on West 78th Street of 1886, these remain the exceptions. More often, when town houses in New York looked like their neighbors it was because they were anonymous, contractor-built brownstones. Important houses had to stand out, or how else were people to know that they (and their owners) were important?

That remained the case right through the middle of the twentieth century. The first serious modern town houses in New York, the house designed by William Lescaze for his own use in 1934 on East 48th Street and Lescaze's house of 1941 for Dorothy and Edward Norman on East 70th Street, true to their modernist roots, were designed to stand out crisply from their neighbors, not to blend in. (That more than half a century has made both of them seem almost quaint, and as much a part of tradition as any of their houses beside them, neatly exemplifies a paradox of modernism at this moment in history almost everywhere.) So, too, with Philip Johnson's Rockefeller Guest House, a Miesian essay of 1950 on East 52nd Street, and Paul Rudolph's elegantly composed, black glass Hirsch house of 1970 on East 63rd Street: they are both exquisite objects, sharply differentiated from everything around them.

Is there an American equivalent to John Wood's great Royal Crescent at Bath, perhaps the most lyrical town house grouping ever created, or to the groupings by John Nash at Regent's Park and elsewhere in London, where similar town houses were joined to create a composition of monumental grandeur? Not yet, no. The American town house groupings created in the nineteenth and early twentieth centuries are too marginal, good though they may be; putting the upper classes into identical-looking buildings has never been our stock-in-trade, which is why the Upper East Side of Manhattan, even at its best, was never going to look like Belgravia.

It isn't going to happen now, either; for all our age's commitment to urbanistic values, we haven't come close to finding a vernacular language for our age that possesses the civilizing urbanism of Georgian London. But much of the work shown here makes strong gestures in that direction, and toward balancing individual expression with the sense of the building as part of a streetscape. That is the most encouraging thing of all about the work in this book, even beyond the implicit celebration of the city that all of these town houses represent, since it surely must be said that if there are so many clients commissioning so many serious architects to build new town houses, then people must be believing in the city as well as in architecture. But beyond this, the architects whose town house work Gorlin has assembled here, like Tod Williams/Billie Tsien, Olson Sundberg, Walter Chatham and Dirk Lohan, all give hope that architects are eager to produce a viable urbanism that does not take refuge in the sentimental and soft solutions of an excessively derivative architecture. They increasingly understand, as Gorlin himself proved in his Corbusian villa at Seaside, that modern, architectural expressions can comfortably coexist with all that is cherished in the traditional city, and even make it stronger.

Philip Johnson, Rockefeller Guest House, New York, 1950

ALEXANDER GORLIN

parallel walls : the new american town house

Within the past ten years there has been a resurgence of the town house. The retreat from the central city to the suburbs has abated and the return to the urban core has been accompanied not only by the restoration of derelict structures but also, surprisingly, by much new construction. This renewed interest in living in the spaces of the traditional city has ironically allowed a reinvestigation of the town house type, abandoned by modernism for so long (although it once was a central focus of activity by architects such as Le Corbusier during the initial rise of modern architecture in the 1920s). This trend is not limited to cities like New York, where the town house was already established, but has also emerged in places like Dallas and Denver, where there never was a dense center. The desire for pedestrian-scaled places to live, where people interface with computers and each other and are free from dependency on the automobile, was also a response to the introduction of the problems of the central city into the suburbs. The ideas of Andres Duany and Elizabeth Plater-Zyberk and the research of the Institute for Architecture and Urban Studies in the 1970s were valuable for their reintroduction of the idea that a city grows, not fully formed from the head of Zeus, but within a set of restrictions that, when properly applied, encourages creativity rather than stifling the new. As opposed to the limitations of pattern book places like Disney's Celebration, the lessons of the development of London, Paris, and New York demonstrate that urban codes and rules have absorbed and encouraged variety and innovation in the creation of the city.

The town house is one of the basic building blocks of the city. Defined by two parallel walls and vertically oriented circulation, it is commonly three to five stories tall, the maximum comfortable climb by a person. It is therefore a housing type intimately related to the human size and scale. The town house is both an individual actor on the stage of the street and also a replicable unit that can be combined to make urban configurations that extend the plan of the city. It embodies many important issues concerning architecture today—the obligation of architecture to the city; the nature of that urban presence; the relationship of the city to suburbia; the tension between the public, exterior facade on the street and the private, interior domain and the correlated formal issues of the facade, wall,

screen, transparency, translucency, luminosity; and the making of plans that are also models for housing at a larger scale—all within the formal typology of the prismatic box, the "most difficult" of the four types characterized by Le Corbusier, but the one he called "most satisfying to the spirit."[1]

The town house is a typology of enormous restrictions, and therefore a laboratory of creative possibilities within a very limited realm. The parallel walls that define the town house type were established by certain structural and economic considerations that allow only a few options regarding circulation, floor area, entry, and functional organization. And yet some of the greatest houses of the last two centuries have been town houses, such as Sir John Soane's house, built in London in the early nineteenth century; the Maison de Verre by Pierre Chareau, built in Paris in 1931; and Le Corbusier's town houses: Ozenfant, Cook, and Planeix. The latter were built despite Le Corbusier's polemic against the very urbanism of the street that the town house implied. Le Corbusier wrote in 1929, "The street is a drain, a deep slit, a narrow corridor . . . the street wears us out, finally it disgusts us."[2] Today no one calls for the destruction of the central city and praises the superhighway as the correct scale of the future as Le Corbusier did, or desires a dispersal of the city into a suburban sprawl, as Frank Lloyd Wright endorsed. On the contrary, the city is acknowledged once again as a locus of creativity, the place of social interaction where there is the call for a "culture of congestion,"[3] to use Rem Koolhaas's term. The avant-garde position in architecture now espouses the human-scaled city.

The form and organization of the contemporary American town house is derived from a multitude of sources: ancient Rome, the London house, the French *hôtel particulier*, and their offspring in the work of the modern masters Soane, Chareau, and Le Corbusier, as well as examples in the United States. Important to the selection of projects in this book is that they be urban and modern (in the sense of a critical reinterpretation of the type rather than a traditional copy from the past). Essential to the idea of a pedestrian-oriented city that is not incompatible with modern architecture is the realization that Classical or Victorian Gothic are not the only good styles, a stance that opposes some of the rhetoric of the New Urbanism. The typology of building does not dictate style, as the traditionalists would have us believe.

In discussing the town house as we know it today, it is important then to begin with the Roman town house as described by Vitruvius, the best examples of which are preserved in Pompeii.[4] They define the type with such precision that they are also praised at length by Le Corbusier in *Towards a New Architecture*. He saw the houses of Pompeii as excellent examples of the possibilities of an animated architecture within a very confined space, as well as having larger urban implications. They fit within the grid established by the north-south axes of the *cardo* and *decumanus*, the cross axis that orients the

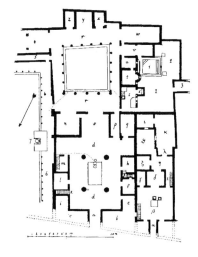

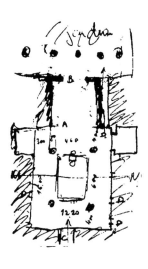

top: View of atrium, House of the Silver Wedding, Pompeii

left: Plan, House of the Silver Wedding, Pompeii

right: Le Corbusier, Plan sketch, House of the Silver Wedding, Pompeii

Roman city. A hierarchy of place is created in which the city is organized around the open space of the public forum as the private house is planned around the atrium and peristyle garden. Incorporating the idea of standardized parts, the Roman house was representative of a type that flourished across the empire.

Characterizing the Roman town house were a number of elements that remained constant but could be varied in plan. A wall defined the street front, often with shops backing onto the house. The entrance vestibule created a transition from the street to the domain of the house, leading to the *fauces*, or "throat," that opened onto the atrium, a high central space, often with an open skylight that collected water into the *impluvium* in a pool below. On axis with the front door was the *tablinium*, either the master bedroom or a depository of the family records, and the most important room of the house. The peristyle garden, surrounded by a portico, lay beyond and was the ultimate focus of the house, completing the metaphorical transition from the city to the countryside in an architecturally rich setting of modulated shadow and light. As Le Corbusier described: "Again the little vestibule which frees your mind from the street. And then you are in the atrium; four columns in the middle (four cylinders) shoot up towards the shade of the roof, giving a feeling of force and a witness of potent methods; but at the far end is the brilliance of a garden seen through the peristyle which spreads out this light with a large gesture, distributes it and accentuates it, stretching widely from left to right, making a great space. Between the two is the *tablinium*, contracting this vision like the lens of a camera. On the right and on the left two patches of shade—little ones. Out of the clatter of the swarming street, which is for every man and full of picturesque incident, you have entered the house of *a Roman*."[5]

The House of the Tragic Poet in Pompeii features an unusual asymmetrical plan, a device that would become important for future interpretations of the town house. Again, Le Corbusier writes: "And here in the House of the Tragic Poet we have the subtleties of a consummate art. Everything is on an axis, but it would be difficult to apply a true line anywhere. The axis is in the intention, and the display afforded

by the axis extends to the humbler things which it treats most skillfully (the corridors, the main passage, etc.) by optical illusions. The axis here is not an arid thing of theory; it links together the main volumes which are clearly stated and differentiated one from another. When you visit the House of the Tragic Poet, it is clear that everything is ordered. But the feeling it gives is a rich one. You then note clever distortions of the axis which give intensity to the volumes: the central

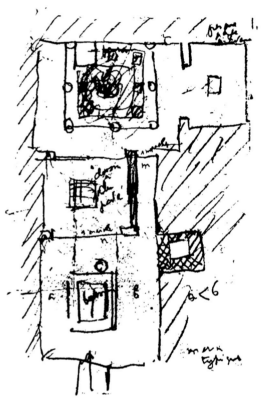

Le Corbusier, Plan sketch of atrium, House of the Tragic Poet, Pompeii

motive of the pavement is set behind the middle of the room; the well at the entrance is set at the side of the basin. The fountain at the far end is in the angle of the garden."[6]

The London town house and its American offspring, in various forms from the mid-eighteenth century to the present day, uses Roman plan elements such as the atrium—often two stories in height—as a means for illuminating the interior, and the similarly organized progression of defined spaces from the street to the garden. For the contemporary architect in particular, it is Le Corbusier's later abstraction and reinterpretation of the classical devices of the London town house that provide the links to the past from which ideas develop in a vocabulary suited to

our time. London is a city of the town house, and the developers who built the city packed as many as possible into the valuable street fronts, as they were responsible for the construction of the street as well. These economic forces and the limit of structural joists to span across the party walls determined the dimensions of the house type. Typically long, narrow lots were laid out, extending back from the street into a garden that was served by a secondary service alley. These "terrace houses," as they were called, sliced through the city at right angles to the street and housed all classes from the poor to the aristocracy within the same architectural typology. As

top: Perspective, Du Cerceau, Pont Saint Michel, Paris

above left: Elevation, Letarouilly, Palais Verospi

above right: Elevation, Letarouilly, Palais Niccolini

below: Elevation, Palladio, town house

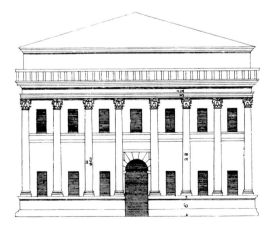

the French writer Louis Simond wrote in 1817, "These narrow houses, three or four stories high—one for eating, one for sleeping, a third for company, a fourth underground for the kitchen, a fifth perhaps at top for servants—and the agility, the ease, the quickness with which the individuals of the family run up and down, and perch on the different stories, give the idea of a cage with its sticks and birds."[7]

The relationship of the levels of the town house to the street was unusual as the street was built up, so that the basement was a half level down. The original grade was maintained only in the garden at the rear of the town house. The custom of building vaults under the house and sidewalk was carried over from medieval times, and a storage area was provided under the sidewalk to the edge of the street. Inside, the plan consisted of one room at the front and one at the rear with a corridor and stair to one side. This was different from the houses on the Continent as noted in Muthesius's *The English House* of 1904, where he remarks that the French and Germans have rooms *en suite*, opening directly onto each other, whereas the English prefer the privacy afforded by a separate circulation zone. In addition, the English predilection for vertical living precluded apartments spread horizontally, which were not introduced to England until 1850.

Andrea Palladio's *Four Books on Architecture* provided an innovative model for the London town house. By joining the portico, previously reserved for the Roman temple and, subsequently, the Church, to the neutral facade of the Italian vernacular farmhouse and the medieval urban home, Palladio revolutionized domestic architecture by giving it a gridded order and dignity with an enormously flexible vocabulary that could be adapted to city or country. Inigo Jones, who visited Italy in 1614 and acquired copies of Palladio's books, was the first to bring the style to England. The sober grid of square windows punched into the plain brick facade characteristic of the Georgian town house was first enlivened with pilasters and set on a plinth in the Palladian

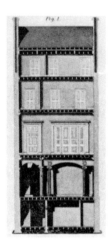

Elevation & section,
First-rate town house

style by Jones in his Covent Garden town houses of 1638. Unfortunately, this aesthetic direction was allied with Jones's patron, Charles I, whose subsequent beheading signaled a political climate that also severed the Palladian style from the facade of the London town house. It was almost a hundred years before the facade would regain any classical embellishment.

The Fire of 1666 burned over four fifths of London and instigated a series of building regulations that did more to determine the vocabulary of the town house than any specific style. Most building regulations in America also came into being after disasters of incendiary origin, such as the Chicago fire of 1871. After the London fire, in 1667, the Act for the Rebuilding of the City of London was passed. Regulating building practices for the first time, the act promoted fire resistant brick and stone for construction, decreed the precise thickness of walls at different heights, fixed the sizes of interior wood joists and ceiling heights, and required that larger houses have first-floor balconies. Houses were divided into four classes "for better regulation, uniformity and gracefulness."[8] Each class was proscribed to be of different heights from two to four stories. Subsequent acts legislated more details. The Statute of 1707 outlawed all wooden eave cornices, substituting stone, and raised a horizontal parapet that hid part of the gable, giving the effect of a flat roof from below. Another law in 1709 pushed the wooden window frames back from flush to four inches behind the face of the brick facade, adding a measure of solidity to the street front. Windows changed from casement to double-hung sash, giving a more uniform look to the elevation. (Many years later, Frank Lloyd Wright would wage war on what he called the "guillotine window" and revive casements both for their ventilating capabilities and for their informal sensibility). Culminating the various regulatory laws was the great Building Act of 1774, which was drafted by Sir Robert Taylor and George Dance. It was far-reaching legislation whose effect was to codify existing tendencies in construction and to decree by implication an

aesthetic sensibility of restraint and plainness. A later generation of Victorians would christen it "The Black Act of 1774" for its almost total banishment of ornament. Four categories or "rates" of town houses were denoted by specific economic values and square footages: the "First Rate" house was more than nine squares (900 square feet) and valued over £850; the "Fourth Rate" house was less than £150 and less than three and a half squares (350 square feet). Different structural requirements governed each "rate" regarding foundations, party walls, and other building components. As John Summerson has pointed out, the act standardized types of houses previously built by speculators and created a straitjacket of uniformity from which variation was difficult. Ornament was constrained to flat incised panels consistent with the prevailing neoclassical style; wood was virtually eliminated and replaced by an artificial stone, "Coade stone"; and bay windows that had once been generously proportioned were now limited to a projection of ten feet or less from the facade. The standardization encouraged an insistent homogeneity and often resulted in a dreadful monotony, which John Ruskin in *The Stones of Venice* decried for the loss of detail, color, and sculpture of medieval street architecture "from the Grand Canal to Gower Street; from the marble shaft, and the lancet arch, and the wreathed leafage, and the glowing and melting harmony to the square cavity in the brick wall."[9]

Individuality was largely confined to the interior under the strictures of the Building Act. The best example of such interior innovation was the house/museum of Sir John Soane, the prominent and inventive architect of the late eighteenth and early nineteenth centuries. His London town house is a self-portrait, an architectural statement of the most personal kind in which Soane's eccentric genius is expressed through a series of spaces that distill many of the great architectural themes of his career while framing his exceedingly strange collection of architectural fragments and furniture. The property included parts of three town houses that Soane had purchased, with his office in the first, Number 12 of 12–14 Lincoln's Inn Fields. Renovated and reconstructed over a period of forty years, the house is a labyrinth of space excavated from within the body of the three adjacent urban structures. The center house, Number 13, completed in 1812, was brought forward from the building line and is faced in white Portland stone, with a tripartite

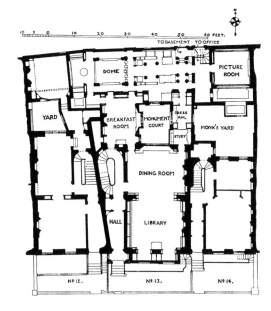

13 Lincoln's Inn Fields (now Sir John Soane's Museum)

left: View of the dome looking east

above: Plan, ground floor, 1837

below: Section, 1827

arch motif in contrast to the more neutral rectangular windows of the two neighboring town houses. Shallow incised ornament crisply defines the plinth of the central entry block that opens up to a series of narrow pilasters on the upper floor to blend in with the adjacent brick facades, perfectly complying with the restrictions on ornament proscribed by the Building Act of 1774. The monumental character of the arched facade is emphasized by two stone sculptures based on the Erechtheum in Athens and Gothic capitals from the fourteenth-century Westminster Hall set into slots between the arches as unstable pedestals rather than as the sturdy base for a lintel above. These act as signs of the two competing styles and moral codes governing architecture in England at the time: the Gothic and the Classic.

One is unprepared, though, for the mad space of the interior, in which Soane explores not only his own dark psyche but also the ancient idea of the house as that space traditionally framing life's passage from birth to death. The plan extends the traditional London town house laterally into two adjacent houses. The resulting "complex" is a manic variation of the Roman atrium house, organized around three courts: the Dome Room, the Monument Court, and the Picture Gallery. In section these spaces break open vertically. Around these main "courts" fragmentary vistas unfold between rooms. On the

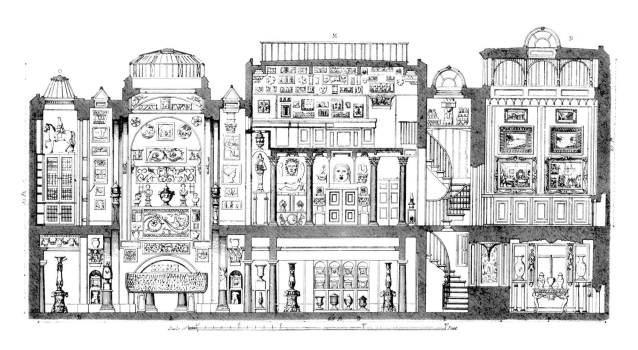

basement level a view down a series of shallow arches alongside an Egyptian sarcophagus evokes the sublime terror of Piranesi's prison etchings. Soane himself said of the vaulted, pavilion-like breakfast parlor, "The views from this room into the Monument Court and into the Museum, the mirrors on the ceiling, and the looking glasses, combined with the variety of outline and general arrangement in the design and decoration of this limited space, present a succession of those fanciful effects which constitute the poetry of architecture." The complex and dynamic interplay between spaces, the sense of being in "rooms within rooms," gives the impression of the house as a microcosmic, domestic expression of the urban scale outside. At the same time, it is also a triumphant dialogue between deeply personal and idiosyncratic interior spaces and a restrained, civically oriented facade, a modern duality that continues to appear in town house design.

When combined in units, the London town house could create urban spaces in squares such as Covent Garden and John Nash's Regents Park. John Wood Sr. and John Wood Jr. created an extraordinary series of urban spaces in Bath, where the town house became the module for the swelling oval of the Circus, the serpentine undulations of Landsdowne Crescent, and the expansive curves of the Royal Crescent. The monumental facades masked fairly ordinary town house plans. The Circus turned the Roman Colosseum inside out with a tripartite facade defining a circular space intersected by three streets. The Royal Crescent was more definitive, with a grand series of Ionic columns atop a plinth supporting a generous cornice and enclosing on one side—only one half of the original design was built—a space recalling the plan of the Colosseum. The sequence of urban spaces, from Queen Square to the Circus to the Crescent, endured as a model for British urban planning until the beginning of the twentieth century.

Curiously, in the newly independent United States there were very few public squares designed with the town house as a unit. Exceptions are Louisburg Square on Beacon Hill in Boston, which was the partially executed plan of Charles Bulfinch; Jackson Square in New Orleans (originally of French origin); Rittenhouse Square in Philadelphia, one of four eight-acre public parks William Penn laid out in his plan for the city; and the squares of various New England towns. Obviously the American Revolution encouraged an independence in the

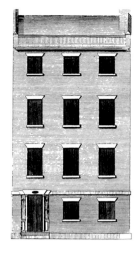
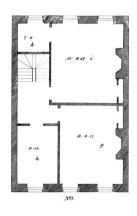
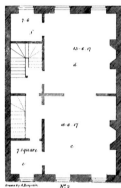
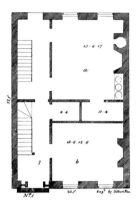

Asher Benjamin, *Elevations & Plans for a Town House*, 1827 edition

new country's thinking about urbanism that distanced itself from the planning of London. However, the pattern had already been set in the older cities of New York, Philadelphia, and Boston to follow the model of the London town house as the example of the standard element of housing in the city. Differences slowly developed, and it took the entire nineteenth century to develop wholly American traditions, which were eventually swept aside with the coming of new architecture from sources as disparate as Frank Lloyd Wright and European modernism. A closer study of the development of the New York town house illuminates some of the immediate background of the emergence of the present American examples.

New York was a Dutch colony until 1664 and derives some of its architectural features from its mother country. The house was raised on a short flight of stairs called a stoop, after the Dutch *stoep*, which allowed a lower basement level to be inhabitable with clerestory windows. This arrangement was similar to the town house in London, where the street itself was built up to provide for light and ventilation to the basement. The stoop gave a monumental character to the modest brick town houses: setting the main level on a plinth gave it more importance and recalled the Italian concept of the piano nobile, which places living areas on the second floor, away from the dust and dirt of the street. The Federal style (1750–1820) was actually Georgian, but after the Revolution this name was not politically correct and therefore changed. It was characterized by a straightforward brick facade, a gabled roof with dormers fronting the street, and a carved wood doorway set in the frame of the brick opening. Inside, on the lower floor, were the kitchen and dining room, with two parlor rooms on the main floor, bedrooms above, and the stair located alongside one of the party walls. The dining room was not brought up to the main parlor floor until much later. Building lots in Manhattan were originally twenty-five to twenty-eight feet wide, but became as narrow as twelve to eighteen feet due to the increase in the cost of land on the island. Stairs in wider lots were originally at the back with a window, but when lots narrowed, the stair was placed in the middle with a skylight above. These houses were often not the work of architects but of builders who used pattern books such as Asher Benjamin's *American Builders Companion* or Minard Lafever's *The Modern Builders Guide*, each with different styles to choose from and including instructions in basic methods of construction. The Federal style was modest in its appearance and presented a sober background as the more dramatic Greek Revival style started to take over.

The narrower lots that were more common by the time of the Greek Revival style

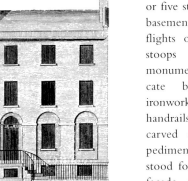

Asher Benjamin, *Elevation for a Small Town House*, 1827 edition

pushed up the height of the town house to four or five stories above the basement level, and the flights of steps of the stoops became more monumental, with intricate black wrought ironwork balustrades and handrails. Elaborately carved doorways with pediments and columns stood forward from the facade as freestanding

elements, and the entry vestibule was pushed deeper into the body of the town house, creating a play of shadow and light with large cornices crowning the roofline above. Henry James described an example of the style, Dr. Sloper's house in *Washington Square*, as "a handsome, modern, wide-fronted house with a big balcony before the drawing room windows, and a flight of white marble steps ascending to a portal which was also faced with white marble."[10] The Greek Revival style eliminated the gabled roof and dormer and substituted a more severe horizontal cornice line.

170 Central Park West, New York, ca.1877

The archaeological and romantic interest in ancient Greece, partially fueled by Greece's struggle for independence from the Ottoman Empire, was expressed in town house design through the focus on the freestanding columns of the entrance portico. This culminated in 1832–33 with Colonnade Row (on Lafayette Street in New York and attributed to Alexander Jackson Davis), which employed a double-height open loggia of Corinthian columns on a one-story-high rusticated plinth. This series of sixteen adjoining town houses was acclaimed as the most magnificent residence in the city at the time, a massively monumental assembly creating a street front recalling the models of Bath and the terraces of Nash in London of 1780s. It also pointed out the general lack of coordinated, street-long town house edifices that were more common abroad.

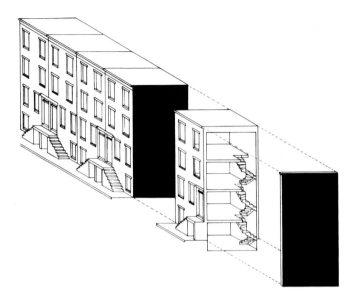

Exploded axonometric, bandbox house, Philadelphia, ca. 1750, drawing by Steven Holl

As in England, the conflict between Classic and Gothic extended to America, however without the polemically charged atmosphere. The Greek Revival eventually succumbed to the darker, more somber tones of the Gothic and Italian Revival styles, which made extensive use of brownstone, a type of sandstone quarried in New Jersey and Connecticut that, when freshly cut, is pink but soon turns brown due to the presence of a hematite iron ore inside. Vincent Scully eloquently summed up the brownstone's appeal: "As the true urban culmination of the century the somber brownstones appeared, stately and marvelous, looming above the iron speared sidewalks, bold and warm in their presences, varied in their forms."[11] Brownstone spread and became the predominant color of New York, beloved by some and despised by others, such as Edith Wharton, who claimed it was "the most hideous stone ever quarried" and made the city "hidebound in its deadly uniformity of mean ugliness."[12]

As the city moved rapidly uptown, with fashionable neighborhoods changing frequently, the styles of town houses mirrored the architecture of the day, reflecting the confusion that characterized the nineteenth century. The public face of the town house was reticent in its immutable mask of conformity and in the subdued Federal style. By the late nineteenth century the display of wealth became an accepted and encouraged attitude in the Gilded Age as reflected in the colonization of New

York's Upper East Side, with Fifth Avenue known as "Château Country." Architects such as McKim, Mead & White and Richard Morris Hunt led the charge, designing palatial French, Italian, and Gothic confections where private luxury was no longer confined to the interior but ostentatiously displayed in the architectural mass and detail of marble and limestone facades. Often entire European interiors were imported and installed to instantly gratify the urge to acquire not only wealth but also culture and taste. This eclectic cacophony lasted until the rise of modernism in the city.

At the same time the town house model was used in a denser and more compressed form, called tenements, for the lower classes. This was as much a consequence of the dimensions of the grid superimposed on Manhattan in 1811 by the New York State Commissioners Plan, where blocks of two hundred feet by eight hundred feet were subdivided into lots of twenty-five feet by a hundred feet. Far from being an act of genius, as Koolhaas wrote in *Delirious New York*, the width of the blocks was too narrow for the necessary service alleys common in grid planning such as in London and Philadelphia. Town houses were built not only for the poor but also for the rich on as much as ninety percent of the lot, squeezing all light and air out of the site. Laws were passed calling for lightwells and minimum distances in rear yards, but a consequence of the block size is that even today many grand Upper East Side town houses built in the late nineteenth century have as little light and ventilation in the rear as tenements on the Lower East Side. Space became the ultimate luxury in New York. This situation lasted until the 1880s when the extreme density and rise of real estate prices started to change New Yorkers' attitudes toward living in apartment houses.

In other cities it was different, with the tradition of Philadelphia's town houses dating back to William Penn's plan for the city laid out in 1685 by the surveyor Thomas Holes. This was soon after the London fire, and from the beginning brick was used extensively as the major material of construction. The

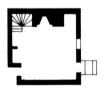

Plan, bandbox house, Philadelphia, ca. 1750, drawing by Steven Holl

large-scale blocks laid out by Penn were eventually broken up into smaller lots with service alleys and led to a type of town house peculiar to Philadelphia called the bandbox, a tower house, with one room per floor, set along secondary streets in courts or mews facing each other, often at the rear of larger houses. As small as sixteen feet square with a winding stair inside, they could be as high as five stories tall. The other common Philadelphia town house type was one room deep and then narrowed to allow a side yard. The stair to the upper level was in a space called a "piazza," and the rear back building, where not developed into bandbox types, became stables. The basement was suppressed in Philadelphia, for the kitchen was deep below grade, and the ground-floor parlor was the most elaborately furnished room in the house.

In Baltimore, a somewhat younger city close to Philadelphia, the town house developed along the same lines and eventually became the predominant type. It was common to see unified street fronts of town houses such as Robert Mills's Waterloo Row of 1816 (demolished) in Baltimore than in other post-Revolutionary cities. The Poppleton Plan street grid of 1812 was more functional for town houses than the New York model of the previous year. The blocks were 350 feet long with service alleys in between rows of houses that marched up and down the hills of the city. From the most modest to the largest, many were distinguished by white marble steps, a simple device that, like Palladio's addition of the portico to the Italian farmhouse, gave great dignity to the house. As Vincent Scully has stated, "the proportions are decisive; the buildings are high enough to give the street a shape, the doors and windows showing the scale of human use, the red brick of the defining walls varying in tone and therefore seeming to flow in and out down the street, the window cornices

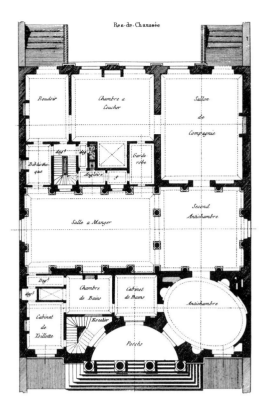

Plan, Claude Ledoux, Hôtel Guimard, 1772

marking a beat, syncopating the rhythm, the major cornices giving the whole street-shape a volumetric definition." H. L. Mencken, a native of Baltimore, called them "those old placid rows" and elaborated, "Why should a man of today abandon it for a house of harsh masses, hideous outlines and bald metallic surfaces. The eighteenth-century house fits a civilized man almost perfectly." [13]

In Boston the Beacon Hill and Back Bay maintain sections with great concentrations of town houses. Asher Benjamin himself lived on Beacon Hill, where many of the town houses, with their swelling curves of bay windows and wooden cornices, were of his design. The architect Charles Bulfinch had planned a large curving square as the center of the Hill. Only partially built, it became Louisburg Square, which is still a magical place, an oasis of green in the midst of the amply curving houses surrounding it on all sides.

In Chicago the fire of 1871 destroyed much of the city, prompting regulations that banned wood construction in the downtown area. Architects rushed to the city, including Frank Lloyd Wright, who built town houses for Robert Roloson in 1894 with steeply gabled ends recalling his own house in Oak Park. Louis Sullivan also came; his houses had sensual, flat ornament that was kept tightly wound to the surface, adorning framed areas. Among the other notable Chicago town houses was Alta Vista

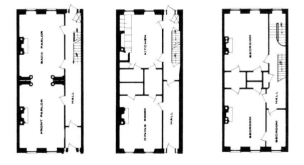

Plans, typical New York brownstone town house

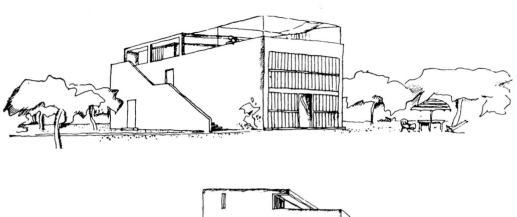

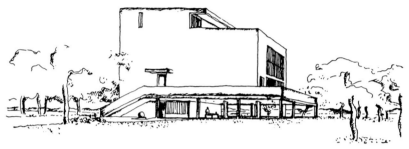

Perspective views, Le Corbusier, Citrohan House, 1921

Terrace of 1900–04, with approximately 480 feet of town houses of divergent styles giving a lively texture to the long facade.

The planning strategies of the Parisian residential models comprise the other significant source of the contemporary American town house today, not so much in relation to the development of the traditional brownstone as to its influence on Le Corbusier and his development of the modern urban typology. The French *hôtel particulier* was originally built to house the nobility in close proximity to the king, but by the nineteenth century the term signified the Paris town house for any class. As opposed to the London town house, the *hôtel* was set back from the street behind a gate and courtyard, with a garden in the rear. Although the facade was usually symmetrical, the plan was not, with unexpected adjacencies and irregularities within the frame of the urban site. This strategy was employed by Claude-Nicolas Ledoux in 1772 in the Hôtel Guimard, where a monumentally symmetrical arched portico is on axis not with the main entrance hall but with the boudoir, apparently in sly reference to Mlle Guimard's reputation as a famed courtesan. Inside, the dining room is sandwiched between the bedroom and bath, inverting and overlapping the private and public spaces of the house. The intricate asymmetries of the *hôtel* often reflected the

convoluted intricacies and intrigues of the French court.

Substantially preceding the categorization of the London town house, the architect Le Muet's seven grades in *Manière de bien bastir pour toutes sortes de personnes* of 1623 standardized the types of Parisian urban houses into a hierarchical typology based on the cost and size of house. It was not unlike seats in the Paris opera, where the width was reduced as one moved further away from the stage (a form of class system still firmly entrenched in the airline industry). The grades (here first grade was the smallest, as opposed to the London system) ranged in size from a tower with

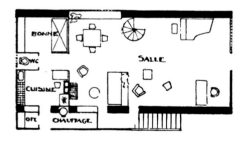

Plan, Le Corbusier, Citrohan House, 1921

one room per floor, at twelve by twenty-one and one-half feet, to a house measuring forty-five by one hundred feet. All of Le Muet's designs are for town houses directly fronting the street, with discussion of the proper furnishing of each room, closets, the placement of the bed, the dimensions of doors, and the height of rooms (thirteen to fourteen feet on the first level, to eleven to twelve feet on the third level). Although there is a basement, it is below grade, not a half level down as in London. Kitchens were on the ground floor, living rooms on the the first, and bedrooms above.

The town house unit provided the module for the construction of two magnificent squares in Paris, the first being the Place des Vosges (Place Royale), constructed in compliance with an order of Henri IV in 1598 that established a code governing the planning of the facades, which would then be built by private individuals after signing leases from the king. Originally planned as a combination of units for silk workshops and houses, the manufacturing aspect of the plan was eventually eliminated, with houses atop a unified, open arched gallery of shops. All of the facades were built to a consistent design, but the plans of the houses extend enormously in depth, merging with the surrounding streets. The houses are wider than most London town houses at forty-eight to fifty-two feet; the roof above was gabled with dormers facing the square. Louis XIV took the concept further in 1686 and built all of the facades of the Place Vendôme (Place Louis-le-Grand) to the drawings of François Mansart, selling the land behind for individuals to build town houses. Even Le Corbusier praised the audacity of the idea, calling the Place Vendôme "one of the purest jewels in the world's treasury."[14]

Le Corbusier's influence on the town house was crucial, though contradictory. Although a master of the type, building at least four in the 1920s (Guiette, Ozenfant, Cook, and Planeix), he excluded the type from his urban plans due to his

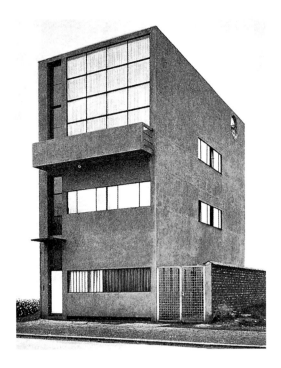

Le Corbusier, view of Maison Guiette, 1926

ferocious, almost irrational, opposition to the street as as a place of "ugliness. . . horror . . . where death threatens us at every step" and "a sea of lusts and faces."[15] He proposed to tear down much of the historical core of Paris (Voisin Plan, 1925), destroying the streets with a vision of isolated towers in an English park setting and lower undulating apartments that opened onto large courts: "The streets of the new city have nothing in common with those appalling nightmares, the down-town streets of New York."[16] The many interpretations of Le Corbusier's plans often became low-income housing projects and the alienating "empty landscapes of psychosis"[17] described by Norman Mailer.

Fortunately, the town houses Le Corbusier built were in fact quite modest in scale and sensitive to the context of the Paris streets in which they were situated. As modern interpretations of the *hôtel particulier*, they were conceptually based on the row house Citrohan type, one of two formal constructs that dominated virtually all of Le Corbusier's work (the other being the horizontal Domino structural system, the basis of the Villa Savoye). In the Citrohan type, a double-height space characterizes the public living areas of the house, and the sleeping areas take up the remaining area of the upper half of this space. Stairs are parallel to the walls, as in the New York brownstone. The piano nobile is open, with living, dining, and kitchen all on one level. Its name being a pun on Citroën, the automobile company that paid for the exhibition of the

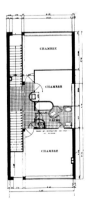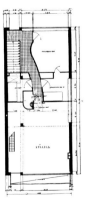

Plans, Le Corbusier, Maison Guiette, 1926

Contemporary City, the Citrohan house was to be like a car, able to travel to different sites. Sketches are presented of the house in the city and on a lake, stretching into the water like a pier.

The Maison Cook of 1926 is raised above the ground for the car to drive underneath, one of the first designs to incorporate the newly invented automobile into the body of the house. Le Corbusier's "Five Points of the New Architecture" are illustrated in the house: the use of horizontal strip windows, free facade, a free plan, roof garden, and the opening up of the ground plane, inverting the classical rusticated base or plinth. The stair is set toward the middle of the plan, and a row of columns marches down the center line, dividing it into two distinct halves in the floors above. The main living area is raised to the second level and is double height, opening spatially to the rooftop garden. A balcony on the roof both juts out to a view of the Bois de Bologne across the street and bulges into the living room as a suspended object. An internal facade is created at a right angle to the street, giving another scale to the interior of the house, in which the living room acquires a more public nature. In all of Le Corbusier's houses, a larger scale is implied, as he conceived of each house as a part of his larger urban vision. The town houses were seen as part of the ideal urban block. In his housing development for Pessac, though, there were a number of freestanding "urban villas" that were actually town houses set apart from one another.

Le Corbusier emphasized the type's parallel walls to direct the inhabitants' gaze, like blinders on a horse, to the view stretched out before them like a flattened canvas. This is evident in the Maison Guiette of 1926, where one of the party walls is set apart from the block of the house with a slot of glass and a balcony inserted in between. The curving walls of the interior play off the stairs, which slide along one wall in a manner that Le Corbusier compared to "Jacob's ladder which Charlie Chaplin climbs in the movie *The Kid*."[18]

left: Pierre Chareau, La Maison de Verre, translucent glass block corridor, 1931
right: Pierre Chareau, La Maison de Verre, detail of steel column and handrail, 1931

The Ozenfant house of 1923 was a studio for the painter Amédée Ozenfant, who was Le Corbusier's partner in the development of Purism, the movement in painting that called for a return to the object, as opposed to the decomposition of analytic Cubism. The house defines the corner of a Parisian street, with a spiral stair coiling up to the piano nobile. Above is the glass cube of the painter's studio with two angled, spiky skylights on the roof. The house has a strangely anthropomorphic, animated character, more like a Cubist portrait of a man smoking a pipe than a Purist still life.

But the masterpiece of the modern town house in Paris is without doubt the Maison de Verre designed by Pierre Chareau in 1931 in collaboration with the Dutch architect Bernard Bijvoet. With the hindsight of history, it is clearly one of the the most influential town houses of the twentieth century and the most extreme, obsessive exploration of the relationship between technology and the sensual domestic interior. It was the home of Dr. and Mrs. Dalsace and also his office. They had bought an eighteenth-century *hôtel particulier* and planned to tear it down and build a modern house, but the elderly tenant who lived on the top floor refused to move, prompting the solution of inserting a new steel framed structure directly below the heavy masonry walls of the apartment above. Within the frame were set panels of translucent glass block, each one square, with a circular lens at the center. As one approaches the house, within the coutyard framed by the masonry walls of the adjacent buildings, it seems to float in a shimmering, aqueous space. The facade appears like an apparition, an evanescent shimmer of glass set within the elegant lines of its steel grid. Two ladders extend the full height of the house with the sole function of holding floodlights to illuminate the glass facade so that the interior glows, day and night, with the *lumière mystérieuse* beloved of John Soane.

Three floors were fit into the space occupied by two floors of the original *hôtel*; As Dr. Dalsace wrote, "the first floor . . . is devoted to medicine, the second floor to social life, and the third to nighttime privacy."[19] Dr. Dalsace's gynecological offices, which look out to the garden in the rear, occupy most of ground floor, with the stair to living area of the second floor sharing the same corridor. A rubber floor, with shallow raised circular discs that match the pattern on the exterior glass block, runs through the offices and the double-height living room. From the inside the glass block affords privacy and recalls Adolf Loos's dictum to Le Corbusier that "a cultivated man does not look out of the window; his window is a ground glass; it is there only to let light in, not to let the gaze pass through." The view is blocked by a cataract of cloudy light, a diaphanous, luminous cocoon, like the dissolved edges of Atget's photographs of the ancien régime. In contrast to the glaze of light at the periphery of the room, one is confronted by the precise industrial details of the structural steel columns bolted together, and the highly articulated black wrought iron cabinets and bookshelves surrounding much of the room. The exposed structure of the steel columns gives the strange impression that they were there before the insertion of the glass house, blurring the distinction between old and new. One entire wall of the living room is devoted to old editions whose texture, along with the wood veneer cabinets, adds a measure of warmth. Sliding partitions separate the main living room from the dining area and views to the rear garden through clear glass panels set into the glass block wall. The Maison de Verre maintains a Japanese sensibility in the translucent panels and the fragmentary views of nature framed in the garden, creating a sense of isolation and apartness from the world, an Occidental reinterpretation of the principle known as *sabi*, seen to greatest effect in the design of the royal Katsura Palace in Kyoto. All around, elements rotate, including the door to the main stair, the wardrobe in the living room, the retractable ladder to the bedroom on the third floor, and the numerous rotating bidets. There are also screens in each of the third-floor bathrooms that rotate around the fixtures to enclose them for privacy and distinction between the room and bath.

Adolf Loos's trenchant writings on architecture reflect a deep meditation on the problem of the house and its implications in an urban setting. He especially touched on the problem of the street-front town house and the dichotomy between the public face and private interior, writing in 1910, "A house should appeal to everybody, as distinct from works of art which do not have to appeal to anyone. . . . The work of art aims at shattering man's comfortable complacency. A house must serve one's comfort. The work of art is revolutionary, the house conservative . . . the house does not have to tell anything to the exterior; instead, all its richness must be manifest in the interior."[20] Loos admired the Georgian

London town house, with its plain exterior and elaborate interiors, praising the facade's "square cavity in a brick wall," which Ruskin so vociferously condemned for what he believed was their unnecessary self-abnegation. Loos's position was

above & center: Plans & section, Adolf Loos, Tristan Tzara House, 1926

below: Adolf Loos, Moller House, interior view to dining room, 1928

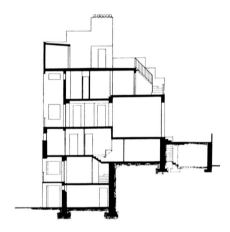

elaborated in the essay "Ornament and Crime," an exaggerated polemic, but one that was nonetheless taken very seriously at the time. "The evolution of culture is synonymous with the removal of ornament from objects of daily use,"[21] Loos wrote in his defense of "naked walls" against the excesses of Beaux Arts pastry cake ornament. His essays and ideas caused a tidal wave of reaction leading eventually to the minimal, flat facades of the International Style. Over a hundred years earlier, in 1774, the London Building Act had the same effect of reducing the town house facades to virtually flat screens.

In his own residential work, Loos struggled between the exigencies of the interior within the restrictions of the prismatic volume, developing the idea of the Raumplan or "plan of volumes." This was a complex internal organization of rooms and circulation in which the demands of each space collided with the symmetry of the exterior. A series of stepped sections created a dynamic and labyrinthine architectural promenade in which spaces bump against each other and views communicate between rooms, recalling Soane's house, where the same effect is created in a classical idiom. In Loos an intense interiority is achieved, where the inhabitant is framed like an actor on a stage, as in the view from the music room into the dining room in the Moller house of 1928. The refracted views in Loos's work emphasize the latent psychological drama inherent in a house, where the unexpected circumstance of meeting on the stair might be the occasion for a scene to be played out between family members.[22]

In a town house this possibility is especially present due to the compression of the parallel walls that act as a literal stage within which all human action takes place.

Loos's town house for the French Dadaist poet Tristan Tzara presents his theories in built form. Facing Avenue Junot, on the hill of Montparnasse, the house presents a massive block with a rusticated stone base containing three rental apartments and, above, a smooth, square stucco facade into which a large rectangular opening is cut, framing a series of smaller windows. The completely symmetrical facade belies the intricacies of the interior, where numerous stairs intertwine and wrap around each other, twisting and turning, encouraging a sense of disorientation and separation from the outside world, and intensifying the private nature of Tzara's abode. The rear of the house steps down in a series of terraces that contrast strongly with the vertical plane of the street facade. Although Loos's interiors are hardly *gemütlichkeit*, they are thankfully not *neue sachlichkeit,* as Loos clearly recognized that the private house was not the place for the clinical objectivity of the International Style as outlined by Philip Johnson in his exhibition of 1929. Loos provides mostly built-in furniture, allowing the space between for the display of the client's "bad taste," as he did not believe in the total control of the architect over the interior.

As European modern architecture spread to America in the 1920s, every domicile from brownstones to châteaux had to pay for their ornamental crimes and were stripped and exposed on the street, becoming bland boxes if they were not torn down entirely to make room for towers in a park. This was the fate, until virtually the 1960s, of the traditional town house, which was unappreciated in all but a few areas, such as Greenwich Village and the Upper East and Upper West Sides in New York, Society Hill in Philadelphia, Beacon Hill in Boston, and parts of Baltimore. On the other hand, due to the basically conservative nature of new residential construction in America, there were very few opportunities for architects to design town houses in a modern vocabulary.

William Lescaze was one of the earliest architects to build a modern town house in New York, in 1937. Causing a sensation upon its completion, it was set within a row of brownstones (described as "dingy" in contemporary articles) with his own office below and the living area on the top floor, like Le Corbusier's Villa Cook, so that it was directly accessible to the roof garden. A glass block front and a curving wall at ground level distinguished it from its neighbors; however, it conformed to the New York City zoning code, and was not set back from the street due to the premium placed on even the slightest plot of real estate. Also in New York, Philip Johnson's guest house of 1949 for the Rockefeller family set a blank brick wall to the street with a Miesian steel and glass cube above. Behind the wall was an open atrium and pond, giving the luxury of space and light within the walls of the city. In Chicago, on University Avenue, Keck and Keck in 1937 built an abstract

Adolf Loos, Tristan Tzara House, view of front facade

above: William Lescaze, architect's residence and office, New York, 1937
below: Keck and Keck, town house residence, Chicago, 1937

hanging gardens. One arrives by elevator to this penthouse extravaganza by way of a translucent white plastic cab decorated with miniature lead soldiers, providing a clue to the strange space to follow. The interior remains one of the more recent and conspicuous examples of a return to the town house as a site of self-reflection in the tradition of Soane: hundreds of cubist mirrors virtually re-create Versaille's Hall of Mirrors on the East River. Light reflected from the river below is used to dazzling effect. The vestibule is a Wrightian compression of space in preparation for the explosion of space and light opening out to the river and expanding in every direction. Certainly outdoing Soane's and Loos's parsimonious use of mirrors, the interlocking puzzle of voyeurism and narcissism approaches rococo excess. A transparent lucite, clear-bottomed bathtub exposes itself to the kitchen below, creating what is surely a strange overhead view for any house. The extraordinary cubic space, with its diagonal views and layered spatial effects, is a kind of glamorous, private folly in the sky.

Hans Hollein also contributed to the New York town house scene in the 1970s with the renovation of the Richard Feigen Gallery. On Seventy-ninth Street the town house facade was stuccoed over with a minimal white surface, relieved only by a double chrome column, looking like elongated cells in mitosis and acting as a cultural sentinel. Remarkably, it fits into the New York streetscape among more staid neighbors and calls out, in a spirit of difference, to the château-style Rhinelander mansion just down the block. Frank Gehry's 1978 proposal for the

brick town house that was a severe structural grid with inset louvers to modulate light. Y. C. Wong's atrium houses of 1960 in Chicago are superb examples of the privacy obtained with a brick wall, each unit organized around an internal garden court. But overall, very few modern town houses were built, as the main thrust of modern architecture's polemic was antistreet, and the town house remained detached from the program of all-inclusive urban solutions. After the early 1950s, though, it became clear that the utopian vision of modern urbanism was no longer an achievable goal; in fact, it often failed with such intensity that many housing projects were literally blown up because they were unlivable and festering centers of crime.

With the eventual return to the city, however, came the concurrent opportunity to build town houses as individual architectural statements. Paul Rudolph's house of the 1970s is as eccentric an investigation of the town house as any since Sir John Soane's. Set atop a brick row house overlooking the East River from Beekman Place in Manhattan, it literally erupts out of the top four floors with cubes of glass, steel, and

Paul Rudolph, architect's residence, views of living room, New York, 1972

de Menil town house in New York is a juxtaposition of inside and outside, treating the house as a box in which the contents have been shaken up. The interior rooms are set at an odd angle to the street and divided into two halves with a bridge between the front and back. The plan is a kind of dislocated French *hôtel*, appropriate to origins of the de Menil family.

With the destruction of many New York town houses before the establishment in 1969 of the Landmarks Commission, a house proposed by Hugh Hardy in 1970 became a cause célèbre due to a bay window that he intended to make just slightly more abstract than its Greenwich Village neighbors. Jutting out at a 45-degree angle, it immediately sent shudders of horror through the newly formed preservation community. In the end it was approved, after Hardy

successfully argued that there had always been a variety of competing, but compatible, architectural styles in the nineteenth century. It was a hollow victory though, as it has become almost impossible to experiment with the town house type, at least on the street front, in New York's Landmark Districts. It is ironic that Lescaze's design of 1937, although now part of the history of the Upper East Side, would certainly not be approved today. One of the ideas of this book is to encourage discussion between architects and the preservation community.

In Chicago, during the 1970s, Stanley Tigerman led the way for a return to the town house in his exhibit "Exquisite Corpse," named after the surrealist game, in which seven architects were to asked to design seven town houses adjacent to each other as an exercise in chance

Stanley Tigerman, Exquisite Corpse Exhibition, ca. 1975

and context. In New York, John Hejduk explored town houses as a mythical return to type in his series of theoretical projects for Venice, Berlin, and Riga, Latvia; variations on this theme were then built in Berlin. Hejduk explored the idea of row houses as individual personalities in conversation with each other. Aldo Rossi also did much to reinvigorate the discussion of the city and the row house in his book *The Architecture of the City*.

The two other directions that gave rise to a new interest in the town house were the closer study of the city by students and architects associated with the Institute for Architecture and Urban Studies who studied high-density, low-rise housing under the tutelage of Kenneth Frampton and Peter Eisenman in the mid-1970s. The other postmodern direction was pursued by Andres Duany, Elizabeth Plater-Zyberk, and Leon Krier, who revived the idea that the form of the city is the result of various codes and regulations that control and determine certain typologies, such as the town house. It was also a reaction to the desertion of the central cities in the 1950s and 1960s and the subsequent demolition of the historic cores such as at Detroit or Newark. Although the lure of the frontier and the open countryside always appealed to the American psyche, the saturation of the landscape has reached crisis proportions: witness recent open space referendums in New Jersey. It was Duany and Plater-Zyberk's idea to create new towns, which would concentrate the population in dense centers in order to prevent urban sprawl. The new town of Seaside in Florida became an experimental community due not only to the proscribed building types but also to the presence of the eccentric developer Robert Davis, who, contrary to expectations, encouraged creative solutions to the code, making Seaside's Ruskin Place the only urban square between New Orleans and Savannah.

The twenty-five town houses featured in this book constitute a wide range in terms of construction methods, materials, and form, but all consistently defer to their parallel walls and explore new possibilities of movement, light, and space within the restrictions of the type. Of primary concern among all of these examples is context and site, though this is not expressed in the literal references to history prevalent during the postmodern period of the 1970s and 1980s. Instead, the modern town house maintains a more subtle and abstract reinterpretation of the surrounding context, as in Schroeder Murchie Laya Associates' Urban Court House, which conflates two great Chicago architectural traditions—Mies van der Rohe's steel frames and H.

John Hejduk, *Riga: Object / Subject*, watercolor on wove paper, 1985

H. Richardson's rusticated stone—and creates a relationship not only with neighboring structures but also with the historical traditions of the city. Current interpretations of the town house also often incorporate the idea of the Roman atrium or peristyle garden, though, again, not necessarily in any literal sense. Steven Mensch's King House in New York, for instance, features a central court with a retracting glass roof. The issue of vertical circulation must always be addressed within the town house typology, which often results in bold stairways that animate the modern town house's architectural promenade. Gorlin's "Stairway to Heaven" House in Seaside, Florida, lives up to its name thanks to the dominant role given to a series of staircases that move up through the house and culminate in open spiral stairs that tower over the house's roof. Another strategy common among the houses in this book is the innovative and unexpected exploration of different materials. Steel often frames wood, resulting in unusual juxtapositions of the industrial with the domestic. Finally, these houses embody the idea of open and loftlike space between the parti walls, creating an architecture that is a physical and perceptual frame for the activities of human life.

1. Le Corbusier, *Oeuvre Complète 1910-1929*, Les Editions d'Architecture, vol. 10 (Zurich: Artemis, 1974), 189.

2. Ibid., 118-119.

3. Rem Koolhaas, *Delirious New York*, (New York: The Monacelli Press, 1994), 125.

4. Vitruvius, *The Ten Books on Architecture*, trans. Morris Hicky Morgan (Cambridge: Harvard University Press, 1914; reprint, New York: Dover Publications, 1960), 176-182 (page citations are to the reprint edition).

5. Le Corbusier, *Towards a New Architecture*, trans. Frederick Etchells (London: John Rodker, 1931), 183-184.

6. Ibid., 189-190.

7. Sir John Summerson, *Georgian London* (New York: Charles Scribner's Sons, 1946), 51.

8. Ibid., 107-108.

9. John Ruskin, *The Stones of Venice* (n.p., n.d.)

10. Henry James, *Washington Square* (1986), 39.

11. Vincent Scully, *American Architecture and Urbanism* (New York: Praeger Publishers, 1969), 83.

12. Edith Wharton, *A Backward Glance* (1990).

13. *The Vintage Mencken*, ed. Alistair Cooke (1990), 202, quoted in Natalie W. Shivers, *Those Old Placid Rows* (Baltimore: Maclay & Associates, 1981).

14. Le Corbusier, *The City of Tomorrow and its Planning*, trans. Frederick Etchells (London: John Rodker, 1929), 152.

15. Le Corbusier, *Oeuvre Complète 1910-1929*, Les Editions d'Architecture, vol. 10 (Zurich: Artemis, 1974), 118-119.

16. Ibid., 118-119.

17. Norman Mailer, "Mailer vs. Scully," *Architectural Forum* (April 1964): 97.

18. Le Corbusier, *Oeuvre Complète 1910-1929*, Les Editions d'Architecture, vol. 10 (Zurich: Artemis, 1974), 136.

19. Marc Vellay and Kenneth Frampton, *Pierre Chareau* (New York: Rizzoli, 1985), 239.

20. Adolf Loos, "Architecture" (1910), *The Architecture of Adolf Loos: An Arts Council Exhibition*, 2nd ed. (London: Arts Council, 1985), 105-106.

21. Adolf Loos, "Ornament and Crime" (1908), *The Architecture of Adolf Loos: An Arts Council Exhibition*, 2nd ed. (London: Arts Council, 1985), 100-103.

22. Beatriz Colomina, *Privacy and Publicity* (Cambridge: The MIT Press, 1994), 258.

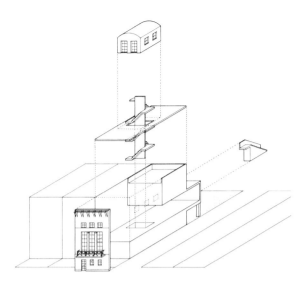

Alexander Gorlin, Eclipse Town House, Seaside, Florida, 1992

Exploded axonometric *(above left)*

Section view of model *(above right)*

Interior view of central stairs *(right)*

Exterior view from Ruskin Square *(below)*

bibliography

Bach, Ira J., ed. *Chicago's Famous Buildings: A Photographic Guide to the City's Architectural Landmarks and Other Notable Buildings.* Chicago: The University of Chicago Press, 1969.

Benjamin, Asher. *The American Builder's Companion.* New York, N.Y.: Dover Publications, Inc.: 1969.

Binney, Marcus. *Townhouses: Urban Houses from 1200 to the Present Day.* New York, N.Y.: Whitney Library of Design, 1998.

Colomina, Beatriz. *Privacy and Publicity: Modern Architecture as Mass Media.* Cambridge, Mass.: The M.I.T. Press, 1994.

Dennis, Michael. *Court & Garden: From the French Hotel to the City of Modern Architecture.* Cambridge, Mass.: The M.I.T. Press, 1986.

Diamondstein, Barbaralee. *The Landmarks of New York II.* New York: Harry N. Abrams, Inc., 1993.

Frampton, Kenneth. *Modern Architecture: A Critical History.* London: Thames and Hudson, Ltd., 1980.

Gallery, John Andrew, ed. *Philadelphia Architecture: A Guide to the City.* Philadelphia, Pennsylvania: The Foundation for Architecture, 1994.

Gopnick, Adam. "The Ghost of the Glass House" in *The New Yorker*, May 9, 1994.

Howland, Richard Hubbard, and Spencer, Eleanor Patterson. *The Architecture of Baltimore. A Pictorial History.* Baltimore, Maryland: The Johns Hopkins Press, 1993.

Huxtable, Ada Louise. *Classic New York: Georgian Gentility to Greek Elegance.* Garden City, New York: Doubleday and Company, 1964.

Iovine, Julie V. "Is There Life After Preservation?" *Metropolitan Home*, December, 1989, pp. 76-79.

Ison, Walter. *The Georgian Buildings of Bath from 1700 to 1830.* Faber and Faber, London, 1948.

James, Henry. *Washington Square.* New York, N.Y.: Penguin Putnam Inc., 1986.

Lockwood, Charles. *Bricks and Brownstones: The New York Rowhouse, 1783-1929.* New York: Abbeville Press, 1972.

Le Corbusier (pseudonym of Jeanneret, Charles-Edouard). *Towards a New Architecture.* A translation of *Vers une architecture* by Frederick Etchells. New York, N.Y: Praeger Publishers, 1972.

— *The City of Tomorrow and its Planning.* A translation of *Urbanisme* by Frederick Etchells. Cambridge, Mass.: The M.I.T. Press, 1975.

— *Oeuvre Complete 1910-1929*, Les Editions d'Architecture (Artemis), Zurich, 1974.

Mayer, Harold M. and Wade, Richard C. *Chicago: Growth of A Metropolis.* Chicago: The University of Chicago Press, 1969.

Mellins, Thomas. "An Architect's Home Was His Modernist Castle: Beekman Place Tower of the late Paul Rudolph is up for sale." *The New York Times*, June 21, 1998, Vol. XI, No. 5.

Miller, Frederic M., et al. *Philadelphia Stories: A Photographic History, 1920-1960.* Philadelphia: Temple University Press, 1988.

Murtagh, William John. "The Philadelphia Row House" in *Journal of the Society of Architectural Historians*, December, 1957, Vol. XVI, No.4., pp. 8-13.

Muthesius, Hermann. *The English House.* A translation of *Das englische Haus* by Janet Seligman, edited by Dennis Sharp. New York, N.Y.: Rizzoli International Publications, Inc., 1979.

Palladio, Andrea. *Four Books of Architecture.* A translation of *I Quattro Libri dell'Architettura* by Issac Ware. New York, N.Y.: Dover Publications, 1965.

Plunz, Richard. *A History of Housing in New York City.* New York, N.Y.: Columbia University Press, 1990.

Ruskin, John. *The Stones of Venice*, edited and abridged by J.L. Links. New York, N.Y.: Da Capo Press, 1960.

Shivers, Natalie W. *Those Placid Old Rows: The Aesthetic and Development of the Baltimore Rowhouse.* Baltimore, Maryland: MacLay & Associates, Inc., 1981.

Safran, Yehuda, and Wang, Wilfried. *The Architecture of Adolf Loos.* London: Arts Council of Great Britain, 1985.

Sinkevitch, Alice, ed. *AIA Guide to Chicago.* New York, N.Y.: Harcourt Brace & Company, 1993.

Scully, Vincent. *American Architecture and Urbanism.* New York: Praeger Publishers, 1969.

Summerson, John. *Heavenly Mansions and Other Essays on Architecture.* New York: W.W. Norton & Company, Inc., 1963

— *Georgian London.* New York, Charles Scribner's Sons, 1946

Stern, Robert A.M., et al, *New York 1900: Metropolitan Architecture and Urbanism 1890-1915.* New York: Rizzoli International Publications, Inc., 1983.

— *New York 1930: Architecture and Urbanism Between the Two World Wars.* New York: Rizzoli International Publications, 1987.

Vitruvius. *The Ten Books on Architecture.* A translation of *De Architectura* by Morris Hicky Morgan. New York, N.Y.: Dover Publications, 1960.

Wharton, Edith. *A Backward Glance.* in Wharton, Novellas and Other Writings, New York; The Library of America, 1990

Williams, Herbert. "The Home of an Uncompromising Modernist" in *Arts and Decoration*, April, 1940, Vol. LI, No. 6

This renovation, which creates a live-in work space atop a five-story town house, turns the usual bulkhead stair inside out and brings the roof area down into the heart of the apartment. Its open atrium is a jewel-like cube of space, defined by copper-lined walls, clear and translucent glass, and bronze windows and doors. A sculptural stair of interlocking cast concrete treads and risers is given an abstract scale through the elimination of a handrail that would betray the intimate size of this space. Fragmented views of the sky and surrounding city, including the looming presence of a large cylindrical

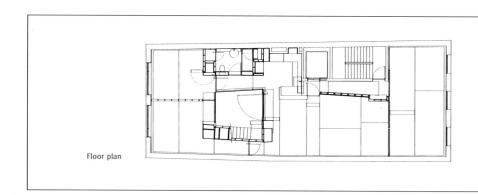

Floor plan

Dean | Wolf Architects **TRIBECA TOWN HOUSE** NEW YORK 1997

wooden water tower, can be glimpsed. The double layers of the glass enclosure create multiple reflections based on the play of images between the interior and exterior surfaces. The space acts like a prism of light in its focussing and refracting the changing hues of the sky.

Strangely enough, although located on the top floor apartment, the space evokes a subterranean dwelling; the ground plane appears to be above, at the roof level. The inversion of the expected gives a mysterious quality to this downtown Manhattan space.

The apartment is zoned carefully between living and work areas with a sliding glass partition between each, which can be reconfigured to allow interpenetration of the two zones. The materials are juxtaposed with precision. The handwrought elements (distressed copper, exposed concrete floors, brick walls, and clear maple paneling) are brought together in a pattern of interlocking rectangles and squares, which continue the idea of the interlocking space of the cube in a two-dimensional manner on the interior wall surfaces.

View of entry hall *(right)*

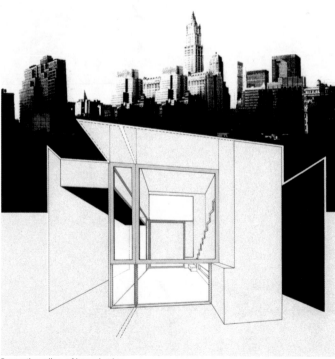

Perspective collage of internal atrium

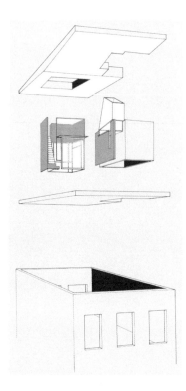

Exploded perspective

Leslie Gill and Bryce Sanders WATROUS WEATHERMAN HOUSE NEW YORK 1998

This residential conversion of a carriage house in Brooklyn Heights creates a completely new interior while respecting the historic shell of the original structure. Within the limits of a small 950-square-foot lot fronting on mid-block mews, living spaces have been carefully zoned to provide areas of dense storage in counterpoint to lofty, interconnected volumes.

The new alteration addresses the front/back split of the house by creating a vertical volume of space that is carried through each floor, running from the entry vestibule to the rear of the lot. This slot of space, a modern interpretation of the traditional brownstone stair hall, responds to the programmatic requirements of the family's needs. The space under the stairs serves as a storage zone, while the area above opens to allow daylight to reach deep into the house. A double-height living space on the second floor provides sectional interest with the two children's rooms on the mezzanine level.

A highly articulated structural system of black steel supports the stairs and landings, framing the space of this seemingly continuous volume and providing an elegant cage-like effect through its linear patterns. A rigorous grid of black iron frames the maple cabinets, and recalls a similar treatment in the Maison de Verre. The bays of the structure provide the primary organization for the space, while regular subdivisions set up a measured rhythm, which extends outward and upward as both a literal module of vertical rods and as a series manifested in the reveals of the cabinetry.

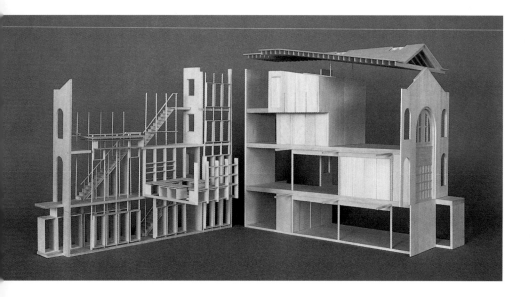

Unfolded plan, section, and elevation *(left)*

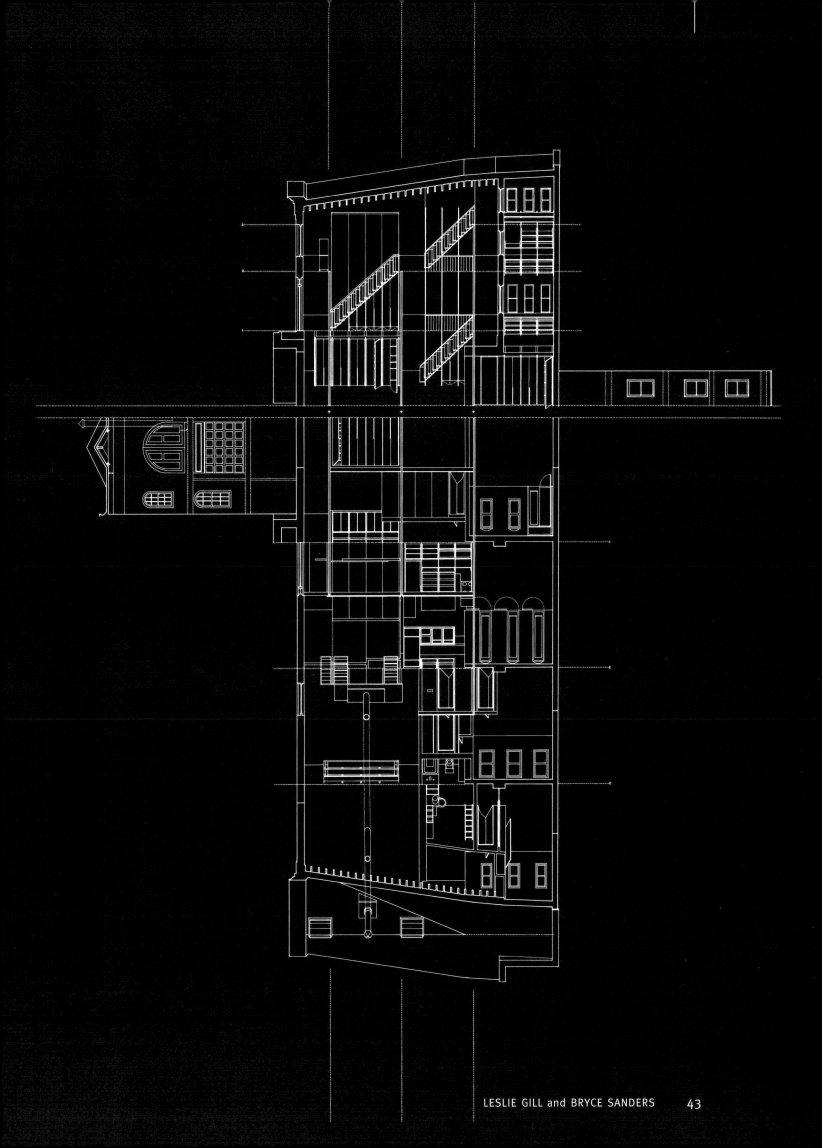

Ground-floor plan

Second-floor plan

Third-floor plan

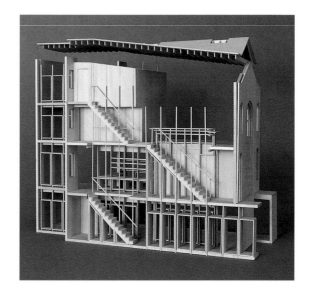

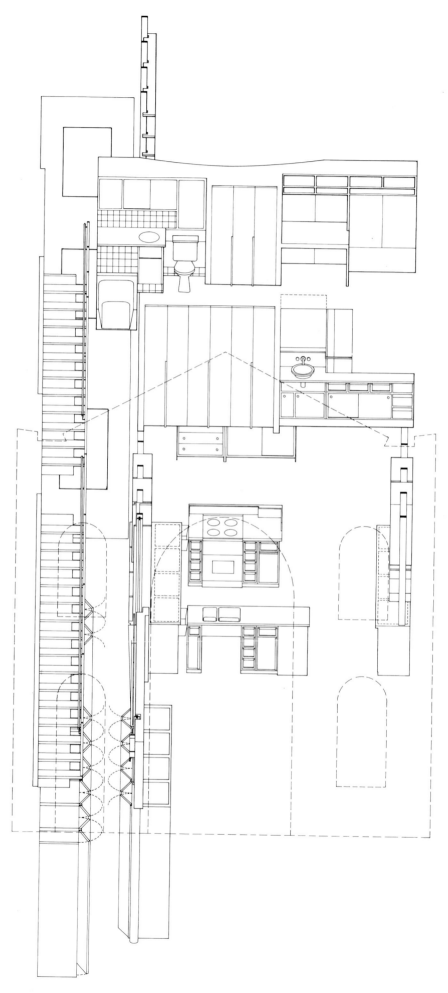

Plan, elevation, and section projection through stairs

This renovation of a thirty-six-foot-wide town house in the Upper East Side Landmark District pulls together a structure that had become a hodgepodge of conflicting additions over the years. The facade, which was previously stepped back in a series of wedding cake sections, was brought forward to the street wall. The paradigm of the classical facade, with its composition of base, middle, and top is reexamined: there is a progression from the heavy stone plinth into a lighter skeletal frame, which includes windows and cornice elements. The facade is faced with a loggia, which serves to buffer the interior from the street. Onyx floors create a suffused glow in the interior. In winter months, the sun warms the air and the internal facade allowing heat to pass into the living spaces. During the summer, the living spaces are cooled by the shadows cast by the sun porch, whose French doors can be opened for ventilation.

reception area to the living room above. Another glass enclosed stair leads from the entrance to the family, kitchen, and dining rooms on the main level. The first two floors are linked to form the public part of the residence, while the third level contains the living quarters for the children, with interior and exterior play spaces. The top two floors contain the master suite and are joined together by a two-story library that acts as a private circulation link. The holly trees planted in the yard create privacy from the adjacent buildings and provide a central open space for relaxation.

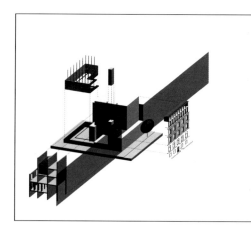

Exploded axonometric

The ground floor is devoted to a gracious entry vestibule and hall that carries through to the double-height glass solarium in the rear garden. A curving wiry stair links the

The sense of interiority that is developed in this town house is remarkable; the grid facade is carried through the space without becoming overwhelming. The internal framed views recall Adolf Loos's ideas about a domestic space, which creates an entire internal world apart from the outside. The architects, in a *Gesamtkunstwerk* manner, have designed all of the house's furnishings—with an interest in the integration of all aspects, ranging from the presence of the house on the street to the fabric on the dining room chairs.

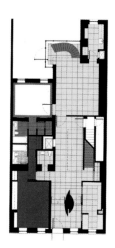

Entrance-floor plan

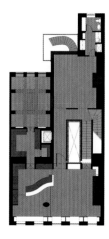

First-floor plan

Second-floor plan

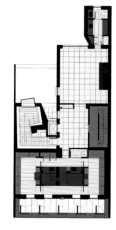

Third-floor plan

Fourth-floor plan

Cross section *(left)*

Hallway off bedroom loggia *(left)*

Though appearing as a romantic ruin of brick arches and open frames against the sky, a completely new interior lies hidden behind the mysterious facade of this West Greenwich Village town house. Entry is through a steel gate and past a ground floor office lit from above by a glass-bottomed reflecting pool, which is the center of the main space above. A narrow brick-lined staircase to the piano nobile of this modern Roman atrium house, where a double-height twenty-by-forty-foot space is framed by a loggia with trees above its ivy-covered walls. The glass roof and side panels retract with James Bond-like drama completely opening the interior to the outside. The living room/studio (at one end of the floor) and the dining room (at the other) are connected by a narrow kitchen. Two children's/guest bedrooms are located on the mezzanine below. Above these is the master bedroom. All three rooms overlook the common garden; the master bedroom also faces the atrium.

The steel structure, following the theatrical character of its intent, is faced with a of thin brick veneer. Full-size brick would have added prohibitive weight, denying the planting of trees above the loggia. Black granite lines all of the floors in the main atrium space, and cast bronze frogs spout water into the reflecting pool.

When all the glass bedroom wall panels are slid open, one is literally suspended between greenery—an experience as far from the density of New York living, where space is at a premium, as possible. This is the ultimate luxury in New York habitation: the enjoyment of space for itself, without the considerations of function and storage.

Steve Mensch Architect   King House   New York   1992

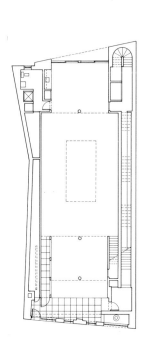

Ground-floor plan

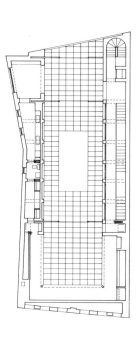

Second-floor plan

This total renovation of a New York town house is a tour de force that completely transforms a traditional nineteenth-century structure into a luminous chalice of light. Restricted by the New York City Landmarks Commission, its simple facade of rectangular windows makes it a modest neighbor along the street. Passing through this plane of limestone, the interior reveals an expansive loft space. The area between the bearing walls provides a strong presence, which leads to the stark minimalism of the walled garden in the rear. A skylit atrium—framed by sheets of transparent and

Ogawa | Depardon HILPERT HOUSE NEW YORK 1998

translucent glass, with wood and aluminum stairs winding upward—floods the interior with light. The closets, mechanical shafts, cabinets, and dumbwaiter are pushed to one side of the floor and placed in a thickened wall, allowing for the maximum openness of plan for the programmed spaces.

Although striking in its form, the program is traditional, with kitchen and dining room on the ground floor, as in the oldest New York town houses; living spaces on the main level; and bedrooms on the upper floors. A very generous master bath takes up the entire width of the street side of the house.

The rear of the town house, with its new full-height extension of glass and steel, is quite different from the adjacent buildings. In this private rear-garden area, no longer confined by the landmark law, the extreme difference between the punctured brick facades of its neighbors and the rigorous grid of glass and steel makes for urban drama of the highest order. This contrast is responsible for the aesthetic power of the building: openness versus enclosure, the radiance of light from glass versus the absorption of light into masonry, and the heaviness of the brick bearing walls versus the light weight of the steel structure. A reciprocal dynamic is achieved between the new elements, whose power is derived from the juxtaposition with the old, and the older features, which are enhanced by the innovations of the newer forms. It is only through the architectural concinnity of these disparate elements that a remarkable structural unity is achieved.

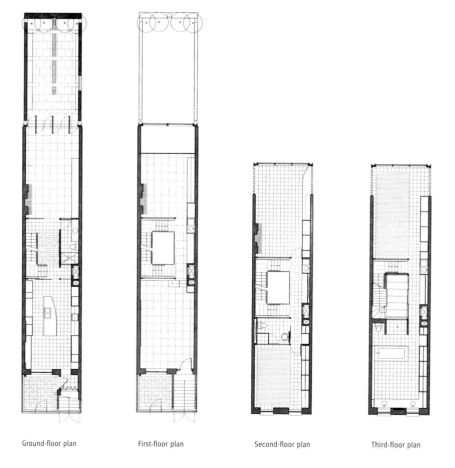

Ground-floor plan   First-floor plan   Second-floor plan   Third-floor plan

Front elevation   Rear elevation

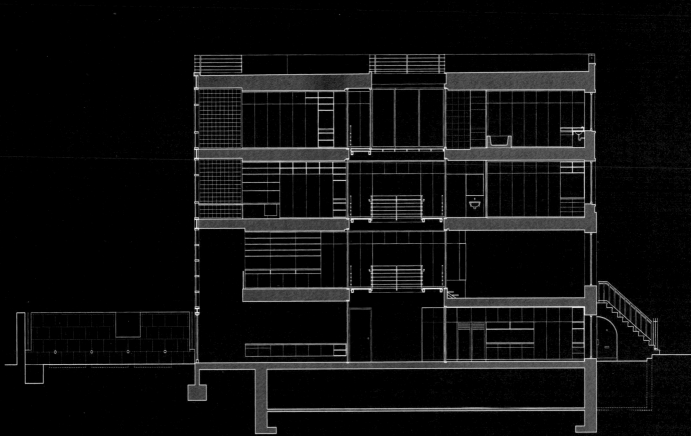

A monumental wall, echoing the front limestone facade, reaches up to a skylight that illuminates the center of the house. A stair winds around this wall from the basement-level pool to the bedrooms on the top floors. The sky is visible from the pool, which reflects light from above. The family, kitchen, and dining rooms are situated on the ground floor, with a bridge to the garden recalling Le Corbusier's Villa Planeix. The living room and study are located on the main level, library on the second, guest room on the mezzanine, parent's and children's rooms on the third, and the staff rooms on the top floor.

The details are brought together through the use of rich materials—cherry or deep green kirkstone floors and glass handrails—which articulate the integrity of each part. The building serves to house an extensive collection of modern art, with many of the walls acting as backdrops for major pieces by contemporary artists.

Tod Williams | Billie Tsien CITY TOWN HOUSE NEW YORK 1997

Set on a thirty-foot-wide lot, this is one of the few innovative, entirely new town houses built in New York in recent years. Its size, detail, and use of sensual materials recall the nineteenth-century luxury town house tradition. Its location on East 72nd Street is an unusual choice—a wide and busy crosstown thoroughfare, rather than a quieter narrower side street where the majority of traditional brownstones have survived.

In order to bring the scale of this six-story town house down to a more domestic level, and in response to the private nature of the program, the central element of the facade, a rectangular, hammered limestone wall framed by translucent and transparent windows, acts as a facade element and screen, providing a sense of protection and privacy from the street. The surrounding glass plane isolates and abstracts the stone wall, while bringing filtered light to rooms within. The rear facade, predominantly composed of glass, is open to the stepped garden in the back of the house.

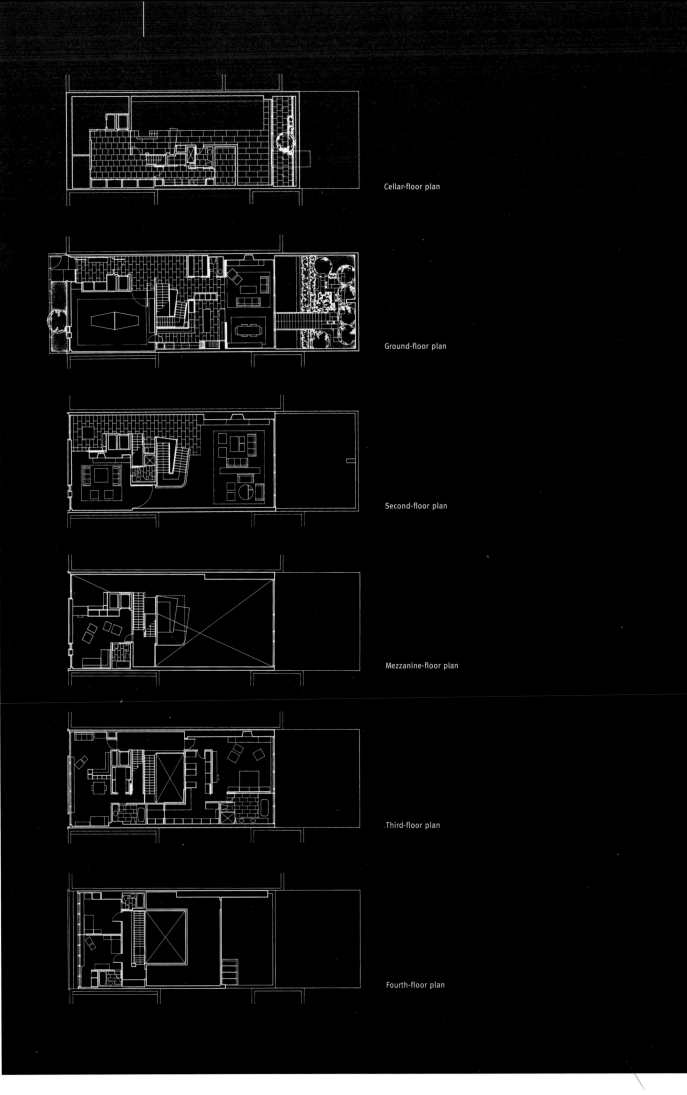

Cellar-floor plan

Ground-floor plan

Second-floor plan

Mezzanine-floor plan

.Third-floor plan

Fourth-floor plan

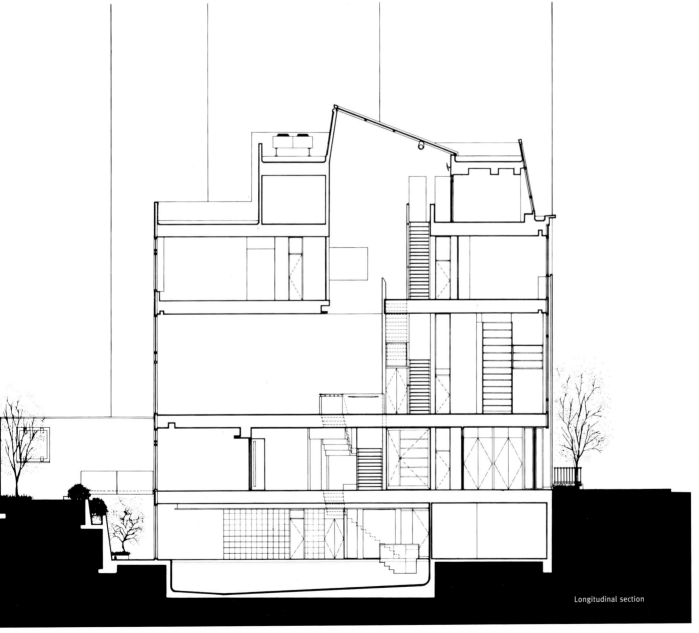

Longitudinal section

This unexpected renovation of a nineteenth-century town house is set in a tightly cloistered court opening directly onto the historic Old North Church of Boston. Three sides of the town house were restored to their original condition, while the south side was literally sliced open. A steel and glass winter garden, which rises to a lead-coated copper balcony, has been inserted in this space. The balcony, spanning both halves of the house, provides views of both the church and downtown Boston. This radical surgery creates a hybrid design of old and new, with each section playing off the

LDA Architects NORTH END TOWN HOUSE BOSTON 1998

other in an internal dialogue of program and site. The traditional garden facade of the town house, where space is usually opened up to the rear, is shifted to the side, along the large brick court of the church.

The ground floor has a bedroom and living space. A spectacular framed view of the spire of the church can be seen from the dramatically rising double-height windows of the second-level kitchen and dining room. A winding stair, placed in the center of the plan, divides the house into front and back sections. The third floor, containing the library and study, is split by a bridge, which spans the open space and allows for views of the kitchen and dining room below. The top floor contains a large master bedroom suite with a balcony. Stairs lead from the balcony to the roof deck.

The extensive use of a modern vocabulary in a historical setting is unusual for this architecturally conservative area of Boston. It demonstrates that new materials and modern syntax are not incompatible with a landmark setting if used with care and sensitivity.

Perspective collage

First-floor plan

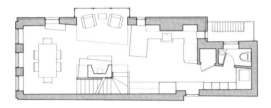
Second-floor plan

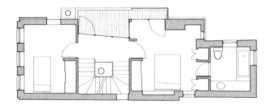
Third-floor plan

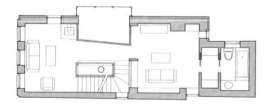
Fourth-floor plan

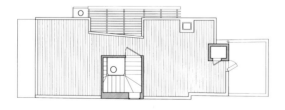
Roof terrace plan

Behind the facade of a town house situated in a historic district of the south end of Boston lies a fifteen-by-thirty-five-foot interior, which has been opened to create a single space. Light from the rear garden streams into the kitchen and dining room on the ground floor. A flight of wiry stairs leads to the second level. A formal entry and living area are completely separated by a bridge that opens up to the ground floor below. A set of stairs attached to the bridge leads to the upper levels: a guest room and area for entertaining on the third floor, a master bedroom suite on the fourth floor, and a roof deck above. Translucent glass walls in the center core of the house by the stair, which are framed by open maple shelves holding a collection of ceramics, allow for the passage of light into the interior. The maple floors and cabinets contribute to the warmth of the space, glowing from the rays diffused by the frosted panels and skylight above. Stainless steel cabinets and countertops characterize the kitchen on the ground floor.

The details of the project have been carefully designed to emphasize the materiality

Christopher W. Robinson LAZ HOUSE BOSTON 1997

of each part. The articulated steel elements of the stairs are painted black, making the maple treads appear to float as if suspended in space. Thin steel horizontal bars topped by a round maple handrail create a spare pattern of line and shadow at the center of the house. The stair is pulled away from the sidewalls to further enhance its sculptural quality.

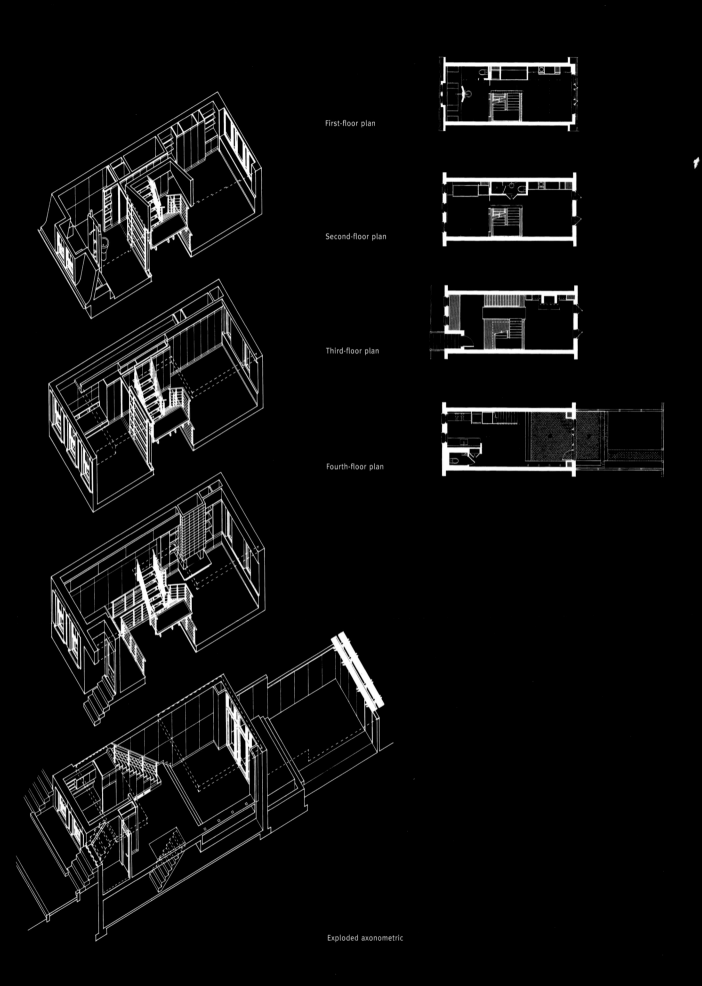

First-floor plan

Second-floor plan

Third-floor plan

Fourth-floor plan

Exploded axonometric

The renovation of the upper two floors and addition of a rooftop room to this town house has been done with an extremely rigorous formal precision, creating a laminated shell inside the masonry brick walls of the original building. Completely open living areas on the top floor are combined with very private enclosed bedrooms on the level below. The narrow corridor of the bedroom level connects a series of rooms, which are mysteriously joined to the ceiling by L-shaped walls, creating slices of light that cut through and separate each space. By taking the normal vertical wall and bending it, an illusion of the walls folding into the ceiling is evoked.

The roof-enclosed portion of the upper level is flooded with light from a large industrial-type skylight. It is completely open, except for an abstract, sculptural kitchen and cabinet construction adhered to the wall of the existing building. The construction is remarkable for its minimal quality, and yet at the same time is engaging, due to a number of asymmetrical shifts and patterns that recall the work of the 1920s De Stijl master Gerrit Rietveld. Planes slip and slide through space, reflecting the light from above in a kind of suspended animation of form.

The third floor room is an urban retreat; access is gained through the roof garden. It is a preserve without telephone, fax, or other forms of communication with the outside world. As a place for reading and meditation, it continues the vocabulary of slipping planes and glass—a fragment of space captured in flux and a pure realization of the dream of light and space open to the sky.

Wesley Wei   TOWN HOUSE PHILADELPHIA 1998

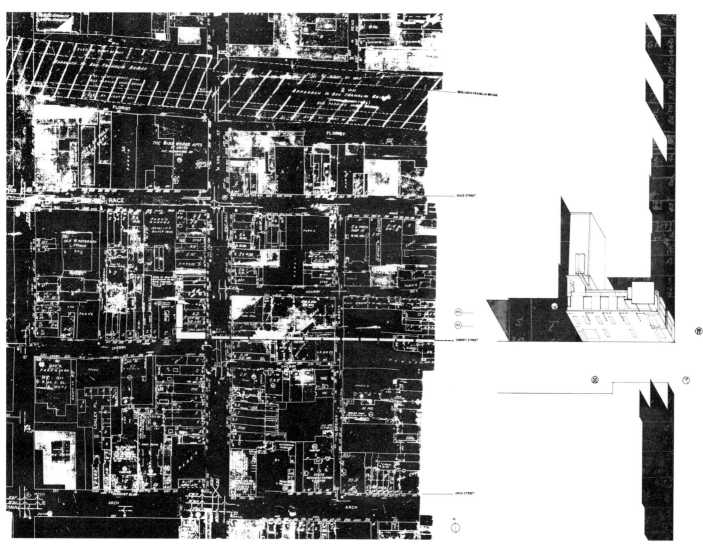

Site plan

Perspective view from street

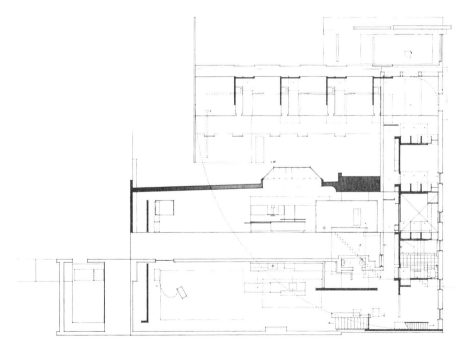

Rotated section & plan

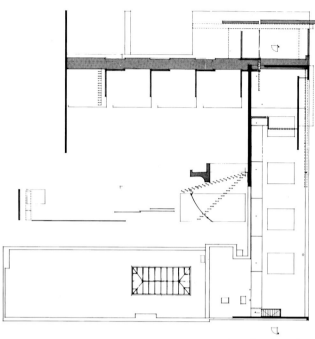

Rotated section & plan

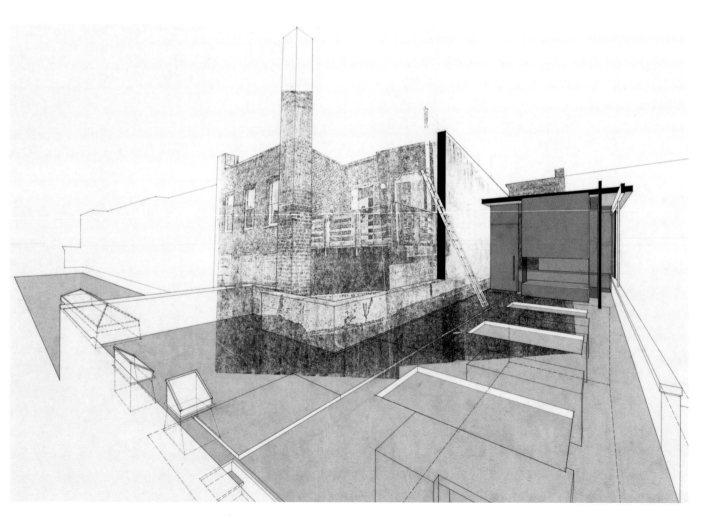

Perspective view of roof pavilion

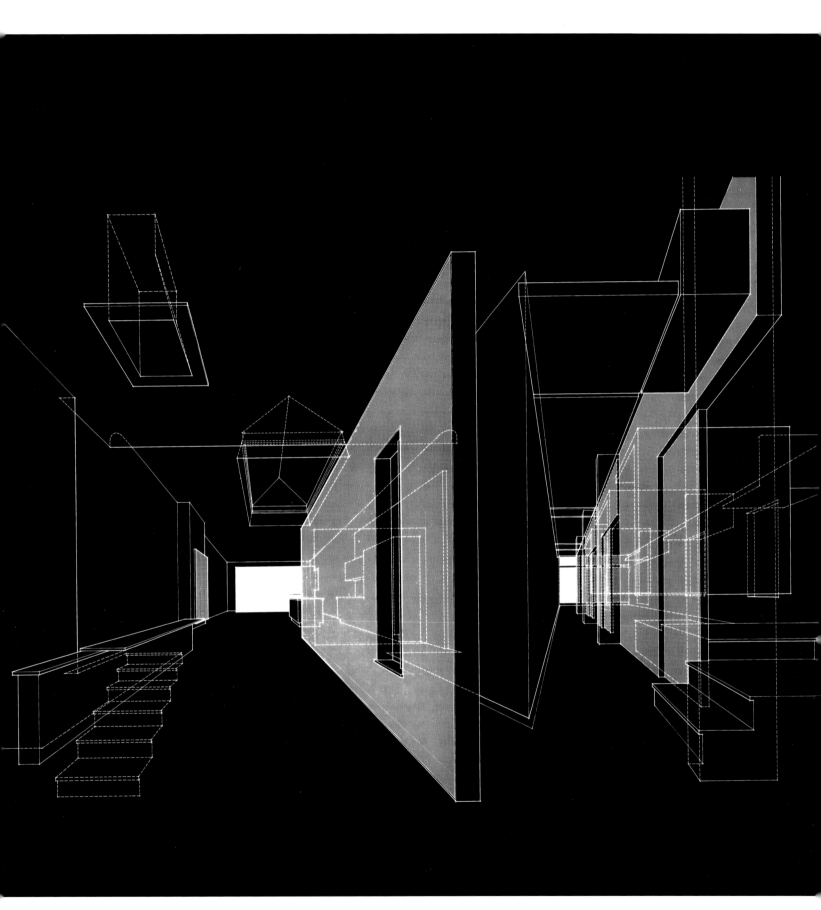

Interior perspective view

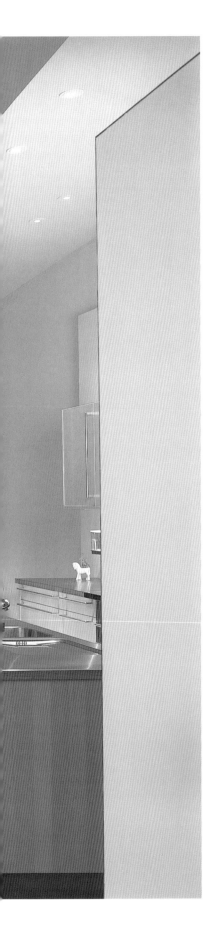

Hallway to bedroom

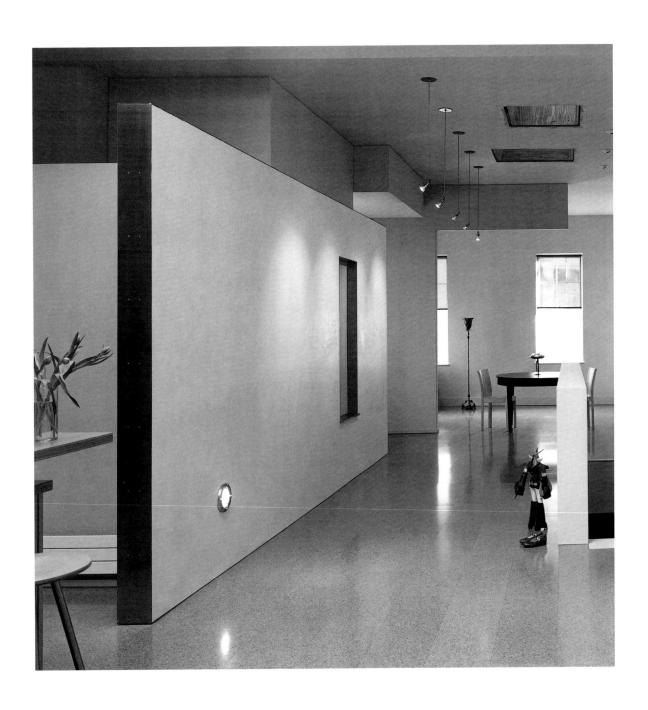

This corner-lot house, the architect's own, and the adjoining neighbor were built at the same time, allowing for experimentation in the creation of two different but interrelated houses. The corner Pugin House has a massive set of side piers, stepped back as less mass is necessary for supporting the bridge-like floors that they span. The piers are clad in stucco and the roof is capped with a corrugated metal vault that gives a slight, coiling tension to the space between these structures. The stairs, plumbing, and service elements are contained within them, completely opening up the

strong presence at the heart of Seaside. It shares the same arrangement of rooms as its neighbor. The upper-level living room is situated near a roof deck, under whose light-weight pergola the waters of the Gulf of Mexico can be viewed. Metal rails are used throughout, including an unusual built-in sag to the ones on the upper deck level.

Across Ruskin Square stands the Forsythe House, a 2,000-square-foot building with a central service core wrapped by stairs and surrounded by open space. Reinforced by steel columns, the core not only forms part

The interior is finished with metallic surfaces, including aluminum paint on the sheetrock around the service core and copper paint on the shingled kitchen walls. The rooftop pavilion is capped with a viewing tower and flag, recalling the nautical references of early modernism.

Combining mass and openness, these town houses were the first to challenge the Seaside building code and reinterpret it in a style different from the prevailing Victorian picturesque.

Walter Chatham   RUSKIN PLACE HOUSES   SEASIDE   1990-1993

center as a loft space. The bedroom and living room are located on the second level, with the kitchen and dining placed on the third level to take advantage of the view and breeze. The interior has a light semi-industrial quality: raw plywood, steel columns, and perforated metal. The brightly colored checkerboard panels are surprisingly reminiscent of the screens in the Katsura Palace in Kyoto.

The adjacent Goodnough House has a grid facade with wooden clapboard filling the side bays and fixed shutters like eyebrows at the one-and-a-half-story height of the upper level. The alternating solids and voids of the facade create a harmonious, if rugged, composition, establishing the building as a

of the structural system but also serves as the sole spatial divider in the building. On the first floor, a studio workshop faces Ruskin Place, and a double-height kitchen and dining space looks out to the alley side. A living room overlooking the space below and two bedrooms are located on the second floor, with a tower room on the roof deck above.

Pugin House *(left)*   Goodnough House *(right)*

Interior of Pugin House *(above & right)*

Forsythe House

This house was conceived both as a critique of the architectural style that has developed at Seaside and an affirmation of its urban code. The abstract vocabulary of the 2,000-square-foot house confronts both the post-Victorian cottage style of Seaside and the classicism of the town houses of Ruskin Place, a pedestrian plaza on axis with the center of Seaside. However, the structure completely conforms to the constraints of the urban code, including its height restrictions and balcony requirement.

In some ways, the uniform urban fabric of traditional styles recalls, albeit distantly, Paris of the 1920s, ready for the emergence of modernism. As a corner unit, the house opens on the diagonal to Ruskin Place. It also faces a small, forested public park. The public gesture of an open stair leading to the second-floor living area recalls both the open loggias of Italian houses on a piazza and the traditional brownstone stoop—a place for casual public interaction. The double-height glass cube of the living area frames a view of the square, and serves as

Alexander Gorlin | STAIRWAY TO HEAVEN SEASIDE 1994

an intermediary zone between the public space outside and the internal private realm. A reciprocal dynamic is at play between the inhabitants on display at the podium and their view of the perambulators out on the square, and the converse; it is a place to see and be seen. At night, the glass cube radiates like the glowing lantern of a coastal lighthouse. An internal facade faces the living room, behind which the master bedroom opens in privacy out to a terrace facing west.

The vocabulary is inspired by the shallow layered space of Cubism. Halls and stairs are threaded through the public and private zones of the house, crossing over from one side to the other, activating spaces through an ascending architectural promenade. The stairs emerge on the roof deck, spiraling up to a crow's nest, which embraces the cosmos and views the horizon of the Gulf of Mexico.

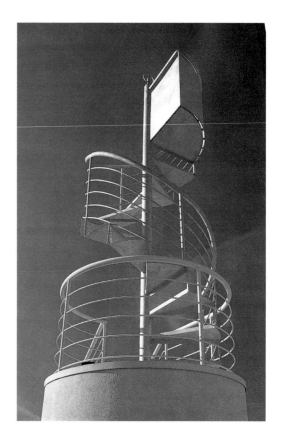

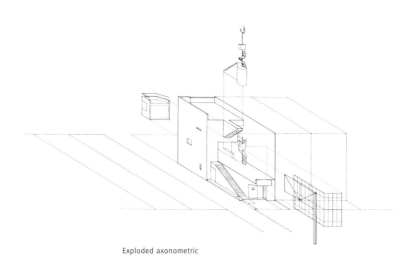

Exploded axonometric

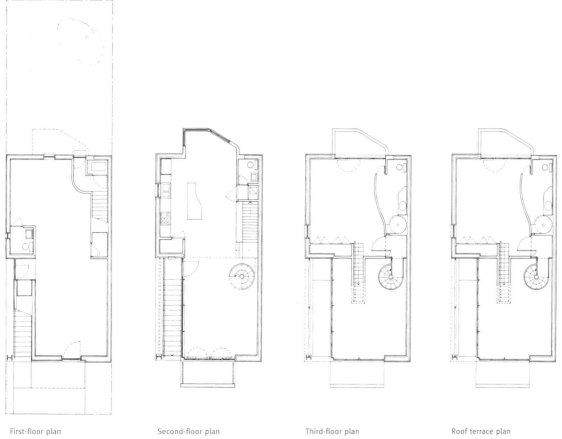

First-floor plan   Second-floor plan   Third-floor plan   Roof terrace plan

This town house on a corner site in Seaside's Ruskin Place is a rigorous interpretation of the vernacular architecture of French Quarter in New Orleans: its exterior facade is composed of oversize French doors framed by plantation shutters.

Like objects in a Giorgio de Chirico painting, the shutters can be manipulated to suggest a range of moods, from the friendly mingling of private and public space when opened, to a surreal and haunting sense of abandonment when closed. Generously sized front and rear terraces underscore the structure's urban

Alexander Gorlin — SHUTTER HOUSE SEASIDE 1996

context while projecting a Creole sensuality characteristic of colonial French architecture.

The light-filled interior is open and loft-like, designed to take advantage of the house's corner site. An open staircase provides circulation from the main living areas on the second floor—the piano nobile—to the bedrooms on the third floor.

A rooftop belvedere commands views of the neighborhood and Gulf of Mexico; its spiral staircase leads to a crowning pavilion that is a stage-like platform for a hot tub. The ascent through the house ends at this grand, outdoor bath—a serene, private sanctuary beneath the sky.

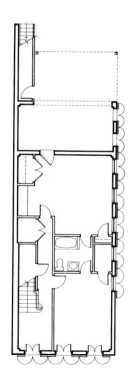

First-floor plan

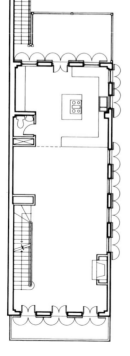

Second-floor plan

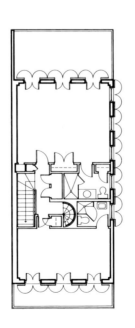

Third-floor plan

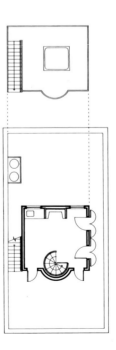

Roof terrace plan

Kettner Row is a series of sixteen row houses built by a developer to help revive a depressed area in downtown San Diego. The houses were conceived to create a flexible living environment whereby portions of each could be sectioned off as rental, office, or loft space, thereby allowing for expansion or contraction based on family or business needs. There are four basic types of houses in the project: the standard row house, convertible row house, apartment over a garage, and triplex. Ten-foot-high garages provide the option of installing car lifts, which allow two automobiles to be parked on top of another.

Jonathan Segal | KETTNER ROW TOWN HOUSES SAN DIEGO 1998

The long row of houses fronting the street is varied through a series of designs and colors, which give a rhythm and texture to the surroundings. All of the units are three stories tall. However, different sections that incorporate double-height living areas and stepped-back terraces add to the interest of the block. Like Addison Mizner's Palm Beach storefronts, they create the impression— though in an abstract manner that utilizes a vocabulary drawn from the International Style—of having been built over a longer period of time. Each unit has a garden that fronts either a motor court or a backyard. The interiors have enormous windows and Corbusian *Citrohan* sections, with kitchens and dining areas below the sleeping chambers. The fifteen- by eighty-foot-long lots enable the narrow units to have natural ventilation and a sizable rear yard. The construction consists of concrete slabs with exposed floors and wood frames with stucco exteriors.

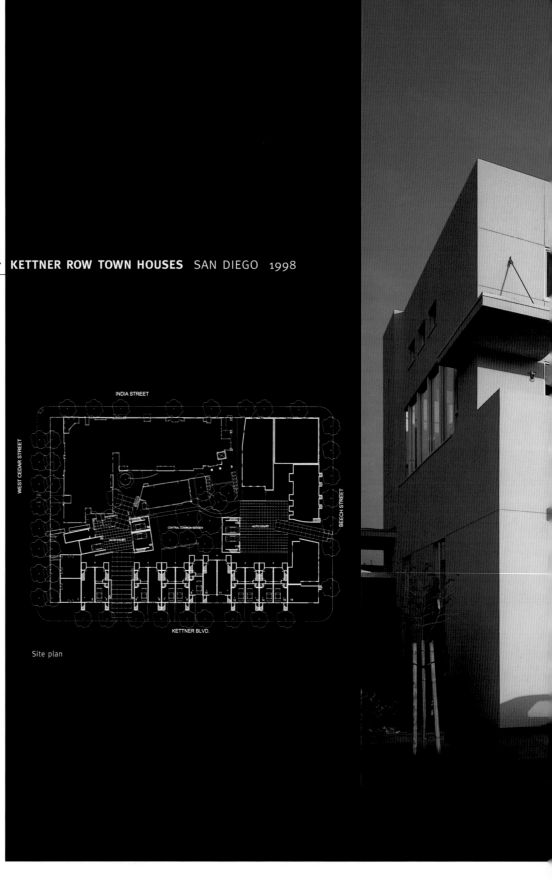

Site plan

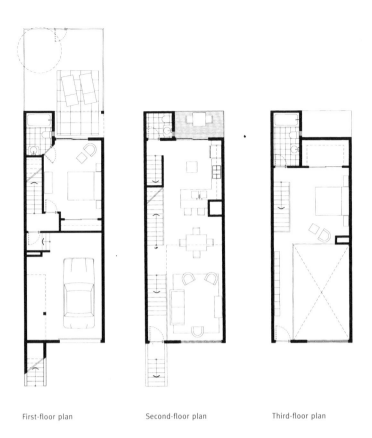

First-floor plan   Second-floor plan   Third-floor plan

These three town houses take advantage of new zoning codes along the Pacific coast in Venice, which allow for denser urban living in what previously had been a more suburban situation. Abbot Kinney Boulevard is a developing community district of artists, designers, and media companies living and working between cafes and restaurants, in the Soho New York style.

Planned for live-in and work arrangements, there is one unit per building; each shares a common vocabulary of forms, colors, and materials, giving the overall appearance of a

A base of exposed concrete block is eroded to reveal a steel frame structure, which borders stucco infill panels of different colors. On the garage-side of the lots, the playfully colored cubes of each unit appear to float above the garage bases. On the other side, the pedestrian entrance, the asymmetrical, L-shaped frames and exposed structure recall R.M. Schindler's work in Los Angeles, a rigorous precedent for urban villas near the Pacific.

Mack Architects ABBOT KINNEY HOUSES VENICE 1997-98

larger development. At the same time, the separate identity of each vertically oriented town house is maintained. Garage spaces and double-height work areas are located on the ground floor. Living areas begin on the second level with open kitchen, dining, and living/work areas opening onto a small internal terrace. The bedrooms are on the third level, with a private terrace looking out to the street. The designation and use of rooms is purposefully vague in order to encourage different options for living and working.

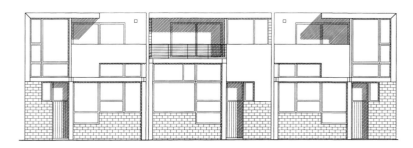

North elevation (street)

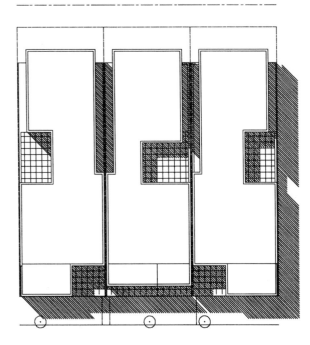

Site plan

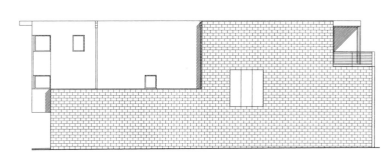

East elevation

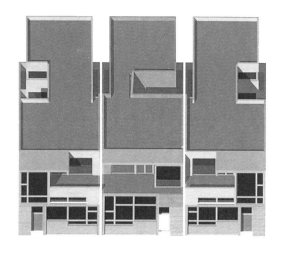

Plan / elevation

Perspective view from street

Perspective view from rear

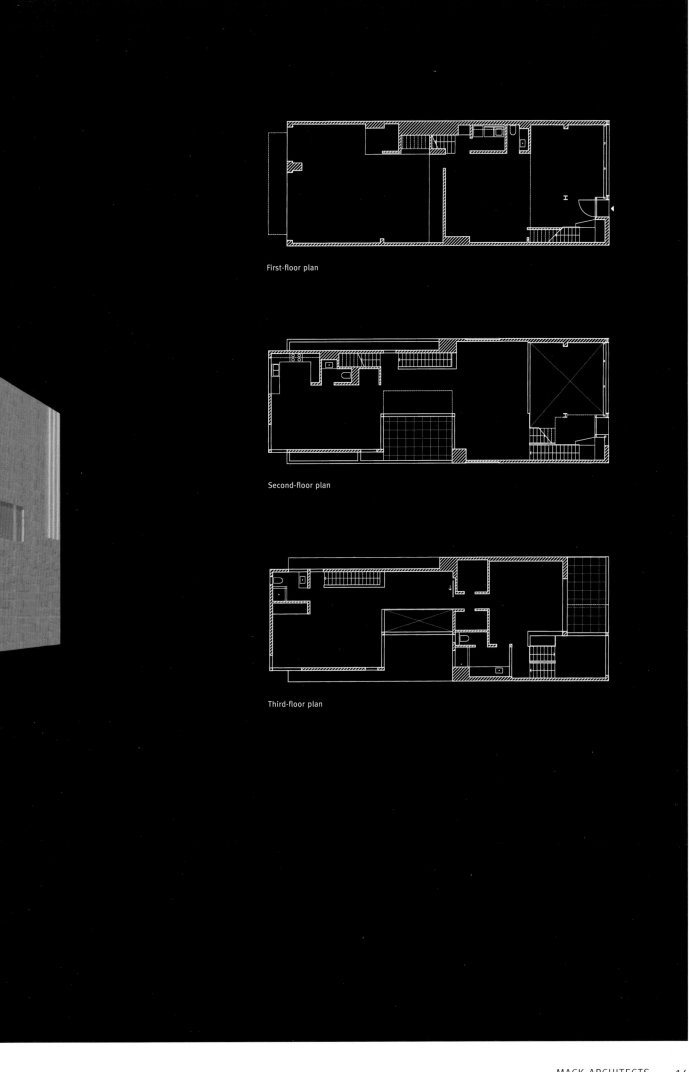

First-floor plan

Second-floor plan

Third-floor plan

Taking its cues from the abandoned art-deco Pepperdine College administration building, this powerful street-front facade gives the impression of having a scale beyond its three-story size. Recalling the Karl Marx Hof in Vienna (worker housing of the 1920s), it has a vertical massing with a repetitive tower-like series of piers that frame five gateways to the individual town house units. At the end of 81st Street is the gate to the central courtyard, an oasis of lawn, palms, and bougainvillea surrounding the open loggias. The towers are banded with small tiles and the tops have vents, completing the image of a cross between industry and deco.

Dan Solomon   VERMONT VILLAGE PLAZA   LOS ANGELES   1998

This project is the winning submission in a design/build competition for a mixed-use development in South Central Los Angeles, sponsored by First Interstate Bank. Vermont Avenue is a three-mile-long abandoned strip of moribund commercial establishments.

The premise of the project is that affordable home ownership is the key to neighborhood revitalization. The plan includes thirty-six full-sized, owner-occupied houses and town houses. Each house has a secured private entry, a private yard or large deck, and two secure parking spaces, which are either private or joined to the garage of one of the other houses. All of the houses and their parking areas are entered from a series of small-scale residential lanes served by the Vermont Avenue frontage road. Private, open space for the street-facing units spans the lanes and forms a series of portals.

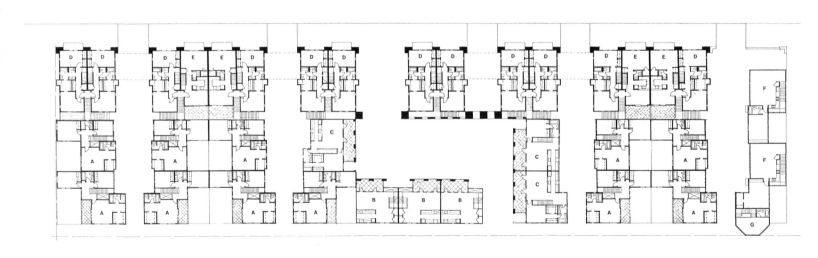

Site plan

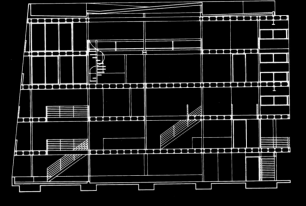

Stanley Saitowitz THE NEW VICTORIAN HOUSE SAN FRANCISCO 1995

Framed by one of San Francisco's hilly streets of bay-fronted Victorian town houses, the metallic, industrial character of this exterior appears at first glance to be in complete contrast to its neighbors. A closer examination reveals that the main facade element, a large projecting bay of horizontal aluminum panels, picks up the rhythm of the adjoining urban fabric. The bay is symmetrically disposed between a steel frame painted Golden Gate red, which stabilizes the building against potential earthquakes and provides a counterpoint to the gray hues of the metal panels. On the left side there are cascading wooden and metal stairs, and on the right side an off-the-shelf series of fire escape ladders.

The bottom three levels are rental apartments that face front and back, each with a stair that connects to the mezzanine levels. The upper two floors are devoted to the architect/owner, with a central double-height atrium over the work space. The interior is constructed of an open web of industrial-style steel joists and wood beams, which are bathed in natural light from the bay window, clerestories, and large skylight. The plan is entirely open, with stairs and services confined to the narrow slots of space on either side of the central open loft areas.

The bay window, whose glass panes and metal bands are set in different sizes, creates a formal ambiguity, which gives the appearance of a building much higher than five stories. Since there is no backyard, the rear bay is sloped to form a light well, which brings sunlight into the interior.

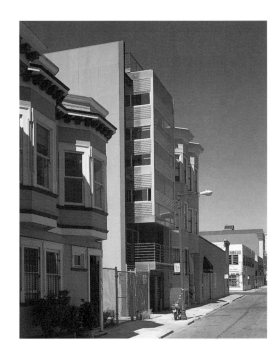

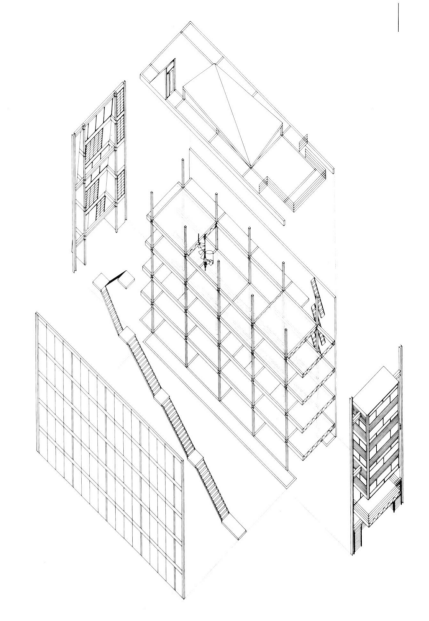

Exploded axonometric

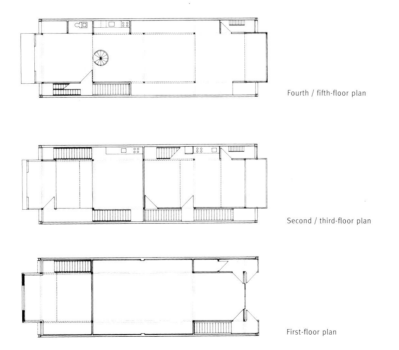

Fourth / fifth-floor plan

Second / third-floor plan

First-floor plan

Though this nine-story, vertically oriented town house extends beyond the general restrictions for the type, it successfully synthesizes the industrial and domestic scales. It appears as a series of town houses along the street, belying its height by an architectural sleight of hand. The site fronts Folsom and Shipley, between Fourth and Fifth Streets. The project has 190 units of live/work and loft-style spaces, parking, and commercial areas on the ground floor.

Embedded in the lower section of the building are four floors for parking, flanked on

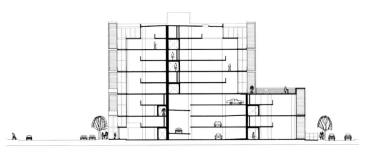

Cross section

Stanley Saitowitz YERBA BUENA TOWN HOUSES SAN FRANCISCO 1998

both Folsom and Shipley Streets by live/work units. A residential tower, set back on the narrow Shipley side, with two-story loft apartments, forms an urban wall along Folsom.

Translucent glass, cube-shaped bay-style windows alternate with carved-out balconies, creating an image that is like an extended town house, four stories higher than the general type. The scale is seemingly brought down by combining the double-height spaces into a single exterior frame. The glass cubes project above the roof, creating a crenelated geometric skyline.

Exposed, post-tension concrete serves as the interior and exterior finish. At night the translucent and transparent glass bays, framed by the concrete grid, are a glowing lantern for Folsom Street.

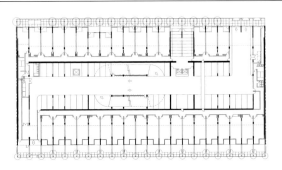

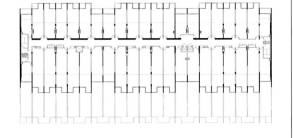

First-floor plan

Typical loft floor plan *(above)* Computer rendering *(right)*

This very tough, spare town house reduces the structural elements to a bare minimum, while creating maximal richness from juxtaposition and the play of light and shadow. The site for this four-level building is a small lot located on a narrow alley in the South of Market district of San Francisco. The clients for the project, a graphic designer and photographer, wanted to combine their residence and individual work spaces within a single, adaptable structure.

piers, which extend forty feet into the sandy in-fill. The piers support a floating, concrete slab at ground level. Steel frames designed both to resist earthquake forces and to visually define the loft zone are bolted to this slab. The frames allow for the open quality of the building's plan and facades. The walls, clear-span floors, and roof are built of conventional wood and plywood framing, designed on a four-foot module.

Tanner Leddy Maytum Stacy **LIVE/WORK HOUSE**   SAN FRANCISCO 1991

The living spaces are vertically stacked in an exposed steel-frame structure adjacent to a narrow stair tower, with the gap between the entrance, marked by a projecting balcony. Recalling Pierre Chareau's celebration of the industrial aesthetic in the Maison de Verre, galvanized sheet metal, cement board, marine plywood, metal mesh panels, and industrial sash windows are assembled within the steel framework. On the interior, a similar attitude toward assembly is employed through the use of opaque acrylic, steel mesh, perforated metal, and other industrial materials. The loft structure design allows for a tremendous increase in the spatial volume and natural light available on this constricted urban site. The graphic design studio is located on the ground floor, behind the garage. It opens onto a garden placed at the rear of the site. The photography studio, which occupies the mezzanine and top floor, has sixteen-foot-high ceilings, skylights, and full-story windows.

Built on land reclaimed from Old Mission Bay, the house is buttressed by concrete

Fourth-floor plan

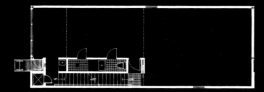

Third-floor plan

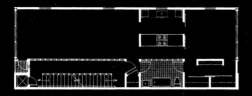

Second-floor plan

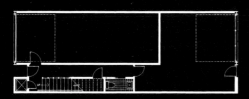

First-floor plan

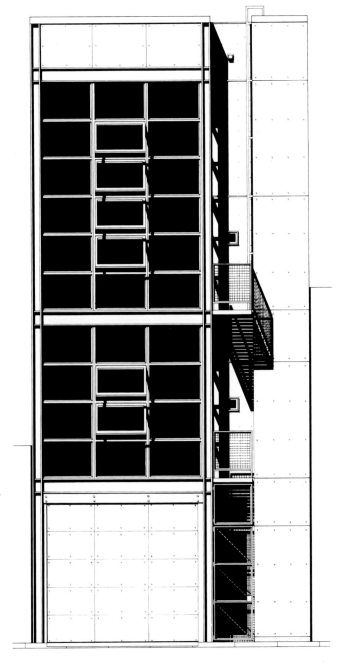

Front (street) elevation

Set atop an abandoned garage structure, this series of recently built town houses blend with their San Francisco Victorian neighbors through an abstract interpretation of the vocabulary of bay windows and cornices. The overall scale of the houses is enlarged and each one is provided with an open, wood trellis, recalling the buzz-cut hippie hairstyle of this cultural locale. The garage base is articulated by the individual character of each unit.

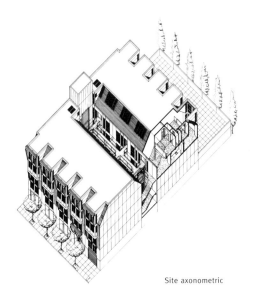

Site axonometric

Tanner Leddy Maytum Stacy **HAIGHT STREET TOWN HOUSES** SAN FRANCISCO 1994

The buildings are entered through gated passageways that lead from the street to the interior courtyard. Each unit faces the court, which acts as a semiprivate space for socializing with fellow residents. A metal-clad stair tower, an open steel staircase, and timber bridges connect the courtyard with the upper stories of this complex.

The individual lofts with their double-height spaces recall Le Corbusier's student housing—a dense beehive of form. Large glazed openings are placed at the ends of the units to ensure ample sunlight and cross ventilation within each unit. The loft plans are organized around a central core containing a kitchen and bath areas located under an exposed timber mezzanine. These plans allow for flexibility of room use and can accommodate a variety of live/work arrangements.

The colorful Haight streetscape inspired the idea of integrating a series of interchangeable, ground-level panels to serve as canvases for sidewalk art. For the first installation, a local artist worked with children to create murals illustrating the history and culture of the neighborhood.

The architectural vocabulary employed here points out a relationship between the native San Francisco structural gothic style and its interpretation in these contemporary works. It proves that it is possible to reinterpret history without resorting to a literal recreation of the vocabulary, which never can exactly capture the spirit of the original.

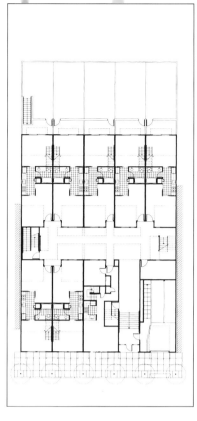

Site plan

Set in the historic center of Denver, down the street from the Beaux-Arts train station, this town house has done much to energize the redevelopment of this previously derelict section of the city. A cubic interpretation of an Italian palazzo and Roman town house, the facade is faced with the red rock sandstone that characterizes the nearby foothills of the Rocky Mountains, giving rise to the name RedHouse. The building establishes a strong urban presence in what is now called LoDo (Lower Downtown). The house also serves as a museum for the owner's collection of pre-

which—alluding to the luxury of Pliny's Laurentine villa, where a series of dining rooms were created for different seasons—offers an alternative setting for taking meals. The master bedroom area overlooks the courtyard. On the third level there is a more intimate gallery and cross-shaped sanctuary space, which sits atop the street-front facade, overlooking the city and court garden with the Rocky Mountains on the horizon. This sanctuary area crowns the building and embodies the themes of heavenly ascension common in the collectors' Spanish Colonial paintings.

Olson Sundberg Architects   LoDo TOWN HOUSE/REDHOUSE DENVER 1998

Columbian, Spanish Colonial, and ancient Greek art.

A massive steel door opens onto a monumental entry hall with a view of an enclosed courtyard garden with a long reflecting pool. The walls are thickened into piers, which define long gallery spaces and enfilades that connect the living and dining areas to the garden. The enclosed garden creates the feeling of being removed from the world, in an oasis of solitude and quiet.

The interior space, with its cross axes and corridors, is an urban microcosm that reflects Denver's city plan in an interior domestic setting. Its vistas are marked by niches for sculpture and art, recalling the monuments that catch the eye at the end of long avenues in the city. A grand stair leads to the second-level private dining area,

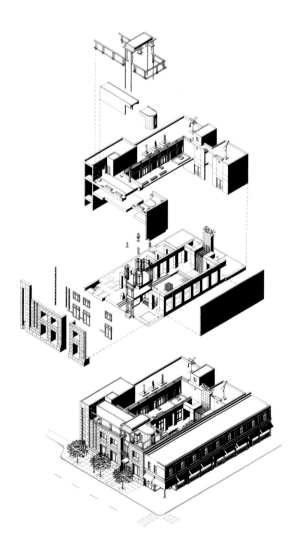

Exploded axonometric

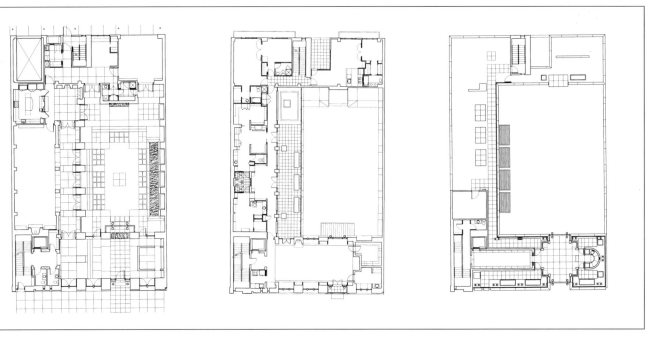

First-floor plan   Second-floor plan   Third-floor plan

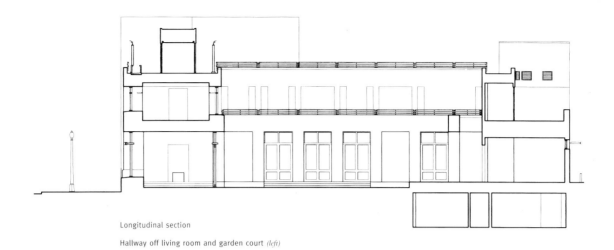

Longitudinal section

Hallway off living room and garden court *(left)*

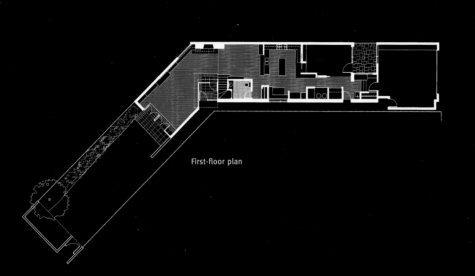

First-floor plan

This house in Chicago's Lincoln Park neighborhood is wedged between three streets and constructed on a dogleg-shaped lot. Although the area is longer than the standard city lot, it maintains the standard twenty-five feet width. Given this restrictive plot, achieving the objective of a sixteen-room house flooded in natural light with large open spaces becomes all the more difficult. While most city houses are sited at the front of the lot with a modest amount of space in the rear, this design inverts the town house typology by pushing the structure as far back as possible. A three-story enclosure

Brininstool + Lynch BRODY HOUSE CHICAGO 1996

Second-floor plan

contains most of the rooms and runs parallel to the back section of the lot, and a walled area in the front creates a landscaped courtyard. The inside angle of the dogleg defines the main entry, the stairway to the second floor, and the media room, which forms a balcony to the living room. The living room turns at this angle.

The large open areas of glass and brick walls follow the stylistic trajectory of the Miesian tradition in Chicago. The interior, on the other hand, provides contrast through the warmth and softness of the wood selected—the grain is used as the intrinsic ornament of the material. The upper-height living room mediates between the garden and the sectionally compressed areas of the house.

Third-floor plan

AMERICAN town house

Brick walls defining the entrance sequence

The exterior austerity of this town house located in a modest Chicago neighborhood belies the richness and complexity of its inner spaces. On the outside, concrete block is the predominant material, interlocking with a weathered wood clapboard cladding. The simple plan—a single run stair on the south wall, kitchen and baths in the core, and rooms in the front and back—is illuminated by an atrium skylight near the center of the block and by two large translucent panels facing south. In order to create a sense of continuity, the concrete block is carried through to the interior and

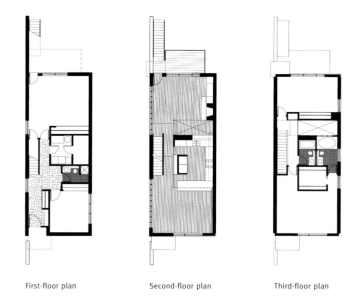

First-floor plan   Second-floor plan   Third-floor plan

Brininstool + Lynch   THOMPSON HOUSE   CHICAGO   1994

combined with the oak floors and heavy grain birch plywood panels and cabinets, all of which add to the warmth of feeling of this domestic space. The grid-bound translucent panels are backlit at night, recalling Japanese shoji panels without literally recreating an oriental interior. Fitting into the grid-pervaded vocabulary of the interior, they also highlight the historical relationship between Frank Lloyd Wright's Japanese sources and the development of modern architecture in Chicago.

The ground floor contains family and study rooms, with service and storage areas. The second floor holds the kitchen, living, and dining rooms, and the master and guest bedrooms are on the third floor. The vertical space of the narrow atrium both adds more light to the interior and provides a counterpoint to the otherwise horizontal spaces of the main level. The house is crowned with a shallow vault that is expressed on the interior bedroom ceilings, the gentle curve relieving the relentless grid of interior spaces.

Longitudinal section

Like a fractured, fissure-ridden cliff face, the facade of this three-story town house located across from Lincoln Park in Chicago is divided into two parts. It is designed to accommodate both a family and an extensive art collection. The massing of the new structure is determined by the historic residence on either side. The facade, consisting of multiple planes of gray granite and glass, achieves a sculptural quality in response to elevations of the adjacent structures.

The main living space is elevated above the street to provide unobstructed views of the park through a special type of glass that is opaque from the outside and nearly transparent from the interior.

The interior is organized around a central stair and atrium, which draws natural light down into the living spaces; it rises the full height of the building and ends at a clerestory that extends the length of the structure. Multiple planes become a back-drop for the artwork, providing a variety of surfaces for display and achieving a dynamic quality in the interior. The furniture has been designed and integrated into the individual spaces to maintain continuity throughout the house at all levels.

Lohan Associates   CHICAGO TOWN HOUSE   CHICAGO   1997

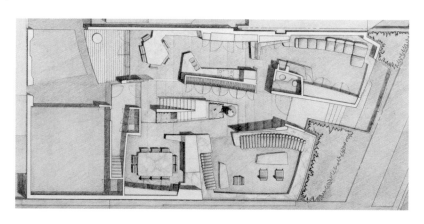

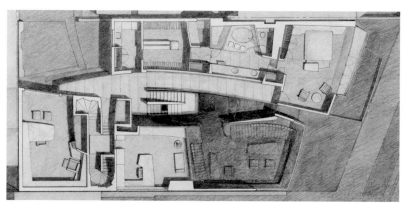

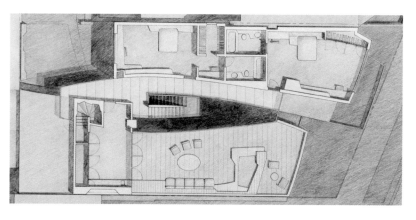

Conceptual floor plans

By combining two great Chicago architectural traditions—the heavily rusticated weight and mass of H.H. Richardson and Louis Sullivan with the steel frame structures reminiscent of Mies van der Rohe—this unique town house acts as a study in contrast and constructs its own history with each section critiquing the other. The rough masonry blocks of the limestone portion of the house relate to the adjacent nineteenth-century building. In what appears to be a completely different building, a grid-shaped steel structure adjoins the stone-faced side and is slightly rotated to enhance the contrast.

Orthogonal to the entry, the house is a series of jumbled cubes, artfully arranged to emphasize the independent room-like nature of each space. Passing through the stone facade, one enters into a cubist explosion of intersecting volumes of gridded and cylindrical space, with hovering planes of transparent mesh and translucent glass block. An enormous variety of spatial variation is achieved within the dimensions of this small space.

The children's bedrooms are located on the second level. A sculptural study is suspended over the living room, with access between achieved by a spiral staircase. The third level holds the master bedroom, with its private deck.

This intriguing idea of placing two totally different styles within the same composition recalls the Gwathmey Siegel renovation of Whig-Clio Hall at Princeton University, where the stylistic opposition brought forth between the old and new elements complements rather than detracts from the overall structure.

Schroeder Murchie Laya Associates STEEL & GLASS HOUSE CHICAGO 1996

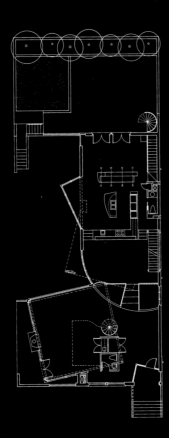

First-floor plan

Second-floor plan

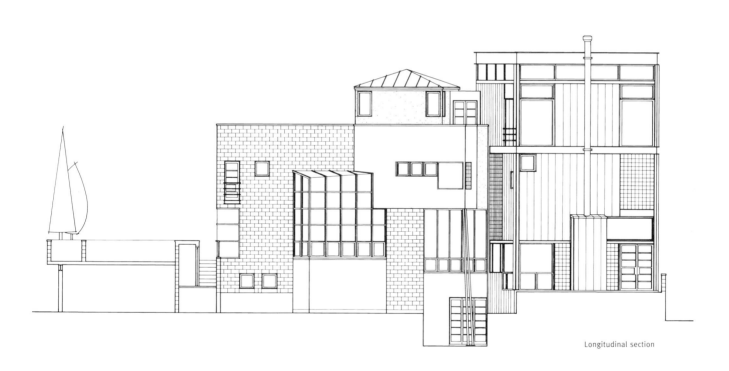

Longitudinal section

project credits

Dean / Wolf Architects; Tribeca Town House
Project Principals: Kathryn Dean, Charles Wolf
Structural Engineer: Anchor Consulting

Leslie Gill and Bryce Sanders; Watrous Weatherman House
Project Principals: Leslie Gill, Leslie Gill Architect and Bryce
Sanders, Bryce Sanders Architecture/Design
Structural Engineer: Aron Rimal, Office of Structural Design

Kiss + Zwigard Architects; Private Town House
Project Principals: Laszlo Kiss, Todd W. Zwigard
Structural/Mechanical Engineer: Adalbert Albu,
AA Architectural Inc.
Interior Design: John Morton Levin

Steve Mensch Architect; King House
Project Principal: Steve Mensch
Structural Engineer: Gary Munkelt
Landscape Architect: Kevin Geround

Ogawa / Depardon Architects; Hilpert House
Project Principals: Gilles Depardon, Kathryn Ogawa
Structural Engineer: Hage Engineering
Mechanical Engineer: Kallen & Lemelson

Tod Williams, Billie Tsien and Associates; City Town House
Project Principals: Tod Williams, Billie Tsien
Associate Architect: Schuman, Lichtenstein, Claman, and Efron
Structural Engineer: The Cantor Seinule Group
Mechanical Engineer: Cosentini Associates

LDA Architects; North End Town House
Project Principals: Treffle LaFleche, Douglas Dick
Structural Engineer: Lemessurier Consultants

Christopher W. Robinson Architect; Laz House
Project Principal: Christopher Robinson
Structural Engineer: Paul J. Donnelly
Interior Design: Louis Laz, Laz Designs

Wesley Wei Architect; Town House
Project Principal: Wesley Wei
Interior Design: Rachael Hoffman Interior Design

Walter Chatham Architect
Pugin House, Goodnough House, Forsythe House:
Project Principal: Walter Chatham
Structural Engineer: Ross Dalland

Alexander Gorlin Architects
Stairway to Heaven:
Project Principal: Alexander Gorlin
Structural Engineer: Sam Johnson
Interior Design: Carl D'Aquino
Shutter House:
Project Principal: Alexander Gorlin
Structural Engineer: Sam Johnson

Jonathan Segal Architect; Kettner Row Town Houses
Project Principal: Jonathan Segal
Structural Engineer: Dodd & Associates
Landscape Architect: Spurlock Poirier

Mack Architects; Abbot Kinney Houses
Project Principal: Mark Mack
Structural Engineer: Parker Resnick

Solomon Architecture and Urban Design; Vermont Village Plaza
Project Principal: Daniel Solomon
Associate Architect: John Maloney
Structural Engineer: G.O. Dyer
Mechanical Engineer: Kalifeh and Associates
Civil Engineer: C.W. Hock
Landscape Architect: GLS Architecture/Landscape Architecture

Stanley Saitowitz Office
The New Victorian House:
Project Principal: Stanley Saitowitz
Yerba Buena Town Houses:
Project Principal: Stanley Saitowitz
Structural Engineer: Watry Design Group
Mechanical Engineer: MHC Engineers
Electrical Engineer: HCP Electrical Consulting

Tanner Leddy Maytum Stacy Architects;
Live/Work House:
Project Principal: Richard Stacy
Structural Engineer: Tennebaum-Manheim Engineers
Haight Street Town Houses:
Project Principal: Richard Stacy
Structural Engineer: Santos & Urrutia
Mechanical Engineer: Brady Engineering
Mural Artist: Michelle Irwin

Olson Sundberg Architects: LoDo Town House/RedHouse
Project Principal: Jim Olson
Structural Engineer: Monte Clark Engineering
Mechanical Engineer: Greenbush Group
Electrical Engineer: Sparling
Civil Engineer: Martin & Martin
Landscape Architect: Ddi Design – Diane Ipsen
Interior Design: Terry Hunziker

Brininstool + Lynch; Brody House / Thompson House
Brody House:
Project Principal: Brad Lynch
Structural Engineer: Stearn, Joglekar Ltd.
Thompson House:
Project Principal: Brad Lynch
Structural Engineer: Stearn, Joglekar Ltd.

Lohan Associates; Chicago Town House
Project Principal: Dirk Lohan
Structural Engineer: Beer, Gorski & Graff
Mechanical/Electrical Engineer: WMA Consulting Engineers Ltd.

Schroeder Murchie Laya Associates; Steel & Glass House
Project Principal: Kenneth Schroeder
Structural Engineer: Stearn Joglekar Ltd.

acknowledgements

I am grateful to David Morton for his encouragement and guidance in support of the concept of this book. The many architects, who have contributed their work, have made this project possible. Damon Ferrante was an excellent textual editor. Richard Hayes contributed greatly with his research efforts at Avery Library. Brendan Cotter's striking design illuminates the idea of the town house. And to my wife, Debby Solomon, for her patience and insights.

index

photography credits